791.4572 STU

Literary Lost

D1440313

Literary Lost

Viewing Television Through the Lens of Literature

by
Sarah Clarke Stuart

continuum

2011

The Continuum International Publishing Group
80 Maiden Lane, New York, NY 10038
The Tower Building, 11 York Road, London SE1 7NX

www.continuumbooks.com

Library of Congress Cataloging-in-Publication Data
Stuart, Sarah Clarke.
Literary Lost : viewing television through the lens of literature / by Sarah Clarke Stuart.
    p. cm.
Includes bibliographical references.
ISBN-13: 978-1-4411-4080-7 (hardcover : alk. paper)
ISBN-10: 1-4411-4080-8 (hardcover : alk. paper) 1. Lost (Television program) 2. Television and literature. I. Title.
PN1992.77.L67S78 2011
791.45'72—dc22   2010033018

ISBN: PB: 978-1-4411-4080-7

Typeset by Pindar NZ, Auckland, New Zealand
Printed and bound in the United States of America

Contents

Acknowledgments

I am deeply grateful for the enduring support of my parents, Susan and Gary Clarke.

I also want to thank the Department of English at the University of North Florida, especially Linda Howell, whose support and encouragement paved the way for this project.

Above all, I would like to acknowledge my favorite *Lost* fans, Steve and Alexis, for their dedication and patience. Thank you.

Introduction: "What, Don't You Read?" *Lost*'s Literary Influence

In the end, Desmond's copy of Our Mutual Friend serves as portal, allowing access to the rest of the fictional world outside the island and to the extended paratextual world that makes up the show's complicated reception as a social text.
— *Steven E. Jones, "Dickens on Lost"*

Even casual viewers of the popular television series *Lost* are likely familiar with its frequent literary allusions and penchant for book cameos. Some of the more dedicated fans know that Desmond Hume has "read everything Mr. Charles Dickens has ever written — every wonderful word" ("Live Together, Die Alone"), and that Sawyer can quote Steinbeck at length. Others might recall the scene in which Benjamin Linus and Jack Shephard discuss a Dostoevsky line; or remember Mr. Eko carving biblical passages into his walking stick, or Juliet Burke engaging in a heated dispute about the literary value of genre fiction.

The creators of the show spend a notable amount of time and effort identifying and addressing other texts and older narratives. Canonical works of fiction appear on screen to underscore an episode's thematic concerns; their appearances, along with other modes of literary citation, provide *Lost*'s viewers with a fresh means of interpreting the televisual text. The allusions invite viewers to initiate a discussion of the show in a more compelling manner than the average "water cooler talk," creating active audiences and expanding "participatory culture"[1] to a new level. Within the realm of their own story, several characters read, discuss and directly quote other stories from a variety of genres and media including novels, plays, fairy tales, films and television shows. This book will focus primarily on the literary references, though at times the references transcend the medium of books.[2]

Viewers of *Lost* have long recognized the series' literary meta-narrative or self-reflexive commentary. *Ulysses, The Invention of Morel,*

Notes From Underground, The Third Policeman, Everything That Rises Must Converge, Our Mutual Friend and *Catch-22* are just a few of the serious works of fiction with brief but noteworthy periods of screen time within the diegesis of *Lost*. The writers also incorporate literary quotes from well-known books like *Animal Farm* and *Moby Dick*. The references, whether they appear on the screen, in the dialogue or as appropriated story lines, provide a hint of intellectual heft, as their inclusion assumes that viewers are familiar with particular notable works. The result of this trend leads to a sense of exclusivity among some viewers, but also to an overall elevation of the typical television consumer. As I will illustrate in the pages to come, numerous fans have been inspired to read because of their connection to *Lost*, demonstrating an interesting twist in the history of television watching.

Certainly *Lost* is not the only popular television show that deliberately employs classic literature, but it is distinct in its mode of presentation. In "The Allusions of Television" David Lavery presents a number of television programs including *Lost, Buffy the Vampire Slayer, The Gilmore Girls, Twin Peaks, Seinfeld* and *Angel* that rely on an audience's familiarity with specific works of fiction. One of his most notable examples is *The Sopranos*, with its quotes from works like Shakespeare's *Macbeth* and Yeats' "The Second Coming" (Lavery 2006). But *Lost* viewers were in a unique position in their anticipation of new allusions, knowing that additional texts would be introduced on a regular basis. During its 6-year, 121-episode run on ABC, *Lost* featured more than 70 books, and many of these appearances were announced long before their episodes aired. For instance, before the final season began in February of 2010, Chad Post, who served as an unofficial literary consultant to the *Lost* writing team, announced that the novel *Deep River* would make an appearance, and fans immediately began speculating about its implications for the next narrative twist. This "leaking" of information serves two purposes: it provides the viewer with a kind of "sneak peek" into the workings of the narrative and it also increases his or her dedication to upcoming episodes.

Literary TV?

Literary Lost does not support the argument that *Lost* is literature or that television is comparable in form or aesthetic to literary works. Rather, I am primarily concerned with the thematic similarities between *Lost* and its featured books, as well as some of its literary forebears and generic influences. I recognize that some readers might hesitate at the prospect of television programming as an entryway to literary studies. Attempting to compare notable works of fiction to the messy plot of an episodic mystery adventure dreamed up by a team of collaborators "churning out" stories likely sounds like an examination of popular culture that has been confused with the study of literature. Some readers might point out that *Lost* is a stimulating narrative as television shows go, but still an unabashed franchise, very different from a serious work of fiction. Without doubt, the series is a product of popular culture, but I would remind readers that authors like Charles Dickens enjoyed cult popularity similar to current serial dramas on television, developing his stories in a comparable episodic fashion. However, this work is not a defense of television nor does it attempt to compare the show aesthetically to novels and short fiction or try to interpret the show as a work of literature.

Common thematic concerns, however, are a different matter. *Literary Lost* attempts to provide an examination of *Lost* through other narratives, mostly canonical works of fiction that draw attention to the most significant themes of the series, such as free will, faith, redemption, community and the individual's desire for an external savior. This book simply identifies, describes and briefly explores the books that are featured in the show or implied as comparison texts. It acknowledges *Lost* as a shared cultural construct and urges the reader to consider the series' subsequent legacy as an influence on literary taste in viewers.

"Intertextuality"

Any text is constructed as a mosaic of quotations; any text is the absorption and transformation of another.

— Julia Kristeva

If viewers have learned nothing else about *Lost*'s vast array of literary and pop culture references it's that, taken individually, they sometimes act like red herrings (distractions that seem, at first glance, to be important clues), leading fans down confusing or meaningless interpretations of the show. And yet, they always provide a deeper understanding of the show's themes and characters. Considered collectively, the books help to expand the meaning of the show, which is sometimes a great relief when meaning within the text seems a little thin. Consider this relevant quote from a significant *Lost* reference, in which the narrator of *Heart of Darkness* illuminates the presence of what today we might call "intertextuality,"[3] explaining how a story can benefit from a multiplicity of narrative predecessors:

> The yarns of seamen have a direct simplicity, the whole meaning of which lies within the shell of a cracked nut. But Marlow was not typical (if his propensity to spin yarns be excepted), and to him the meaning of an episode was not inside like a kernel but outside, enveloping the tale which brought it out only as a glow brings out a haze, in the likeness of one of these misty halos that sometimes are made visible by the spectral illumination of moonshine. (Conrad 1995, 335)

It is interesting that Conrad uses the term "episode" here, prefiguring the language and organization of televisual storytelling. Further, it is not far-fetched to compare this description of nautical tale-tellers with television writers, where Damon Lindelhof and Carlton Cuse, the executive producers of *Lost*, are like Marlow, spinning a "yarn" that relies on an impressive fictional mythology as well as an entire library of extratextual material that "envelops the tale." *Lost* fans are conditioned to investigate and reflect on the book and film references, not necessarily because the writers of the show have a long-term plan to pull all of the referential threads together, but because it promotes a broader viewing experience and allows the show's mystery to be "made visible by the spectral illumination" of other narratives.

That most viewers approach a television text with all of their prior viewing and reading experiences in mind is a fairly obvious point. Viewers use the other, older stories to construct meaning from the narrative at hand. Julia Kristeva is generally credited with the term "intertextuality" and so I will use her ideas of this term going forward: "This notion . . . encourages one to read the literary text as an intersection of texts." She describes the interpretative process of intertextuality as "showing how much the inside of the text is indebted to its outside" (Kristeva 2002, 446). To a large extent, most postmodern entertainment relies on the "spectrality" of other texts, stories that inhabit the present text and are reframed in the newer narrative. Thus, *Lost*'s "intertextual" nature is certainly not unique, but its intentional placement of books makes it more than just a postmodern pastiche. For viewers who become readers of its "guest books," *Lost* haunts the older texts, allowing the medium of television to play its own role in the age-old intertwining system of narratives.

In reference to the nature of postmodern television (which is perhaps a redundancy), Jim Collins explains that "The all-pervasiveness of different strategies of rearticulation and appropriation is one of the most widely discussed features of postmodern cultural production . . . the 'already said' is being constantly rearticulated, but from very different perspectives ranging from nostalgic reverence to vehement attack" (Collins 2000, 378). In the case of *Lost*'s hyperconscious literary references, "nostalgic reverence" is usually the motive. The on-screen appearance of a book suggests certain themes, while paying homage to that particular work. Furthering the postmodern understanding of *Lost*, more than one academic observer has identified the "neo-baroque" qualities of the show, using the model that Angela Ndalianis provides in her book *Neo-Baroque Aesthetics and Contemporary Entertainment*.[4] Intertextuality is a central prong of her neo-baroque construct; she explains that a text's allusions create "folds" and a "labyrinthine" impression. "Neo-baroque narratives draw the audience into potentially infinite or at least multiple directions that rhythmically recall what Focillon labels the 'system of the labyrinth'" (25).

But much still remains to be examined in terms of *Lost*'s postmodern identity and the role that "intertextuality" plays in the "neo-baroque" models of television. This book's intention is not to scrutinize this identity, but rather to provide a straightforward presentation of the program's most significant associations with literary texts, whether through a recirculation and appropriation of story lines and dialogue, or on-screen appearances of the stories. *Lost* re-contextualizes these traditional narratives, bestowing new cultural significance on them. In Ndalianis' words, *Lost* refuses to "be contained within a single story structure" (25).

Influence on viewers

Lost as public service announcement

If we were to examine the following lines of dialogue taken from different points in the series, their collective message might suggest that the average person, in the universe of *Lost* at least, regularly reads and appreciates literary fiction, and that those who do not engage in habitual reading are a marginal group.

It's from *Of Mice and Men*. Don't you read?
— Ben, "Every Man for Himself"

I've read everything Mr. Charles Dickens has ever written —
every wonderful word. Every book except [*Our Mutual Friend*].
I'm saving it so it will be the last thing I ever read before I die.
                    — Desmond, "Live Together, Die Alone, Part 1"

I heard once Winston Churchill read a book every night, even
during the Blitz. He said it made him think better.
                                           — Sawyer, "Namaste"

It's not even literature. It's popcorn. There's no metaphor. It's
by-the-numbers religious hocum-pocum.
                                  — Adam, "A Tale of Two Cities"

In this way, the writers of *Lost* construct a fictional universe that doesn't
quite reflect contemporary readership, at least in American society.
Until very recently, US fiction readers have been in the minority.
According to the National Endowment for the Arts, readers of litera-
ture in 2009 showed an increase for the first time in a quarter-century.
Even so, "the US population now breaks into two almost equally sized
groups — readers and non-readers" (Gifford 2009, section titled "A
Tale of Two Americas"). That is quite a few non-readers.

But the creators of *Lost* send a clear message — reading literary
works of fiction is a standard pastime, and those who are active readers are the best thinkers. Sawyer, for instance, is depicted as the most
literate of the characters, despite his coarse demeanor, and he is one of
the few characters who rely on their own judgment, rarely led astray
by external influences. Jacob, an intelligent, sagacious character, likely
thousands of years old, is shown reading a collection of short stories by
Flannery O'Connor. Desmond, a thoughtful individualist, reads works
by Salman Rushdie, Flann O'Brien and Charles Dickens. Benjamin
Linus, known for his cunning sophistication and intellect, can quote
classic literary passages verbatim and has an impressive collection of
books on the bookshelves frequently shown on screen.

Interestingly, two characters not depicted as readers are Jack
Shephard and John Locke, central figures of the story. John typifies
the primitive man, occupied by thoughts of survival, unconcerned
with abstract narratives or theoretical solutions. Jack is initially portrayed as a practical man of action, well educated, but certainly not
refined in his literary sensibilities. This earlier version of Jack is also
not one to enjoy the journey of a story — he is preoccupied only with
his desired destination, leaving him at a distinct disadvantage when

sit comes to finding the right path. In a more explicit message from the creators of *Lost*, co-producer Damon Lindelof discusses his childhood memories of watching Saturday morning cartoons. He recalls that a celebrity would appear on the screen during a commercial break with a book in hand and tell kids that "reading is FUN-damental!" — a typical public service announcement encouraging kids to read. "*Lost* is trying to do that again," admits Lindelof, somewhat wryly, "[by saying] hey, check out this book that Sawyer's reading" (Lindelof, *The Lost Book Club* 2007).

Viewer response

One of the things we've always enjoyed as storytellers is the intentional ambiguity . . . you're asking the audience: What do you think? We want people to turn to the person next to them on the couch and engage them in a conversation.

— Damon Lindelof (in Chozick 2010)

Initially, my motive to begin the project of writing this book was prompted by a fan's desire to extend the experience of *Lost* during a long hiatus between seasons. Approaching this task as something of a "forensic fan," as Henry Jenkins would say, I wanted to examine each book as a piece of evidence and hoped to make profound connections and possibly explain some of the island's mysteries. I was frequently sidetracked, spending months wandering through stories that revealed very little about the show and at times it seemed I was dealing with a set of texts held together by only the tenuous association of being featured on the same television show. But experiencing the full metatextual narrative was ultimately rewarding, especially when I could share it with other fans who have developed communities around the reading of these particular books.[5]

My secondary purpose for this project was to trace the correlation between the show's book cameos and the viewers' reading habits and literary tastes. Questions naturally arose about viewers' growing enthusiasm for literary fiction pointedly in response to *Lost*. Is it really possible for a television show to inspire a measurable portion of its audience to read new or unfamiliar works of fiction? Besides the explicit workings of Oprah's book club, have we seen a more significant influence on readership among television viewers than in the fan base of *Lost*? How much trust and interest must a viewer have in a televisual narrative to begin a new book or reread a classic, something that seemed irrelevant to him or her in high school but now holds fresh meaning? And, lastly, what kind of communities are cropping up as a result of this renewed literary interest? How many "*Lost* book clubs" are out there?

A community of "fan readers"

It is a summer evening in downtown Jacksonville, Florida. The streets are silent but for a small group of people jingling into a bookshop on the corner of Laura and Madison. In a city where most residents do not gather in the downtown area at night, this group disturbs the quiet streets as they assemble for a rather strange sort of book club. They sit around small tables and begin to chat about favorite plot twists, recurring motifs and characters.

After a period of discussion, chairs are scooted away from tables and everyone is up, searching the store. It seems that a scavenger hunt has been initiated and the participants can be seen rummaging upstairs and down for particular books: *The Invention of Morel* by Adolfo Bioy Casares, *Our Mutual Friend* by Charles Dickens and *The Brothers Karamazov* by Fyodor Dostoevsky. What do these books share in common? They were all featured in *Lost*, of course. The book hunters we see here are, first and foremost, dedicated fans of the show, but also students of a community class called "*Lost*: Finding Meaning in a Televisual Narrative."[6]

They are now settled back at their tables in the café discussing Kurt Vonnegut's novel *Slaughterhouse-Five* and the notion of time travel in fiction. "We have always been here in this bookshop having this conversation," one student says, "whatever happened five minutes ago will always be happening. What I'm saying right now, I have already said and always will say," she explains, describing the notion of time as a loop. Some look doubtful, yet everyone is thrilled at the implications of this idea for *Lost*. They continue making connections between Vonnegut's work and other novels, and then to the show, sometimes without distinguishing among the different fictional worlds and the very different modes of narrative with comments like "Desmond perceives time travel like Billy Pilgrim" and "Dr. Moreau is a literary precursor to the Dharma Initiative — scientists experimenting with the curious properties of an island."

This is a diverse group of viewers, to be sure, unlike my typical university classes. There are a few twenty-somethings, a couple of stay-at-home moms, a 13-year-old and his mother, a college kid and her parents, a middle-aged man on disability. But theirs is a common passion: examining *Lost* through an intellectual lens. On this night their excitement stems not only from the devices of science fiction but also from the discovery of intertextuality, the notion that this show is "no narrative island." It owes its devices, story lines and themes to a multitude of stories that precede it. The class is unlocking a great mystery, even if they are not answering the more typical questions posed about *Lost* like "what is the island?" and "why do ghosts appear to some characters and not others?" Instead, they are exploring the delights of storytelling and the narrative connections that span thousands of years and countless forms of media. As one student triumphantly concludes, "*The Odyssey* was the first *Lost*."

A survey and online discussion

In May of 2010, I conducted a survey to measure the extent to which fans have responded to *Lost*'s literary allusions. According to this online survey, viewers from around the world have been influenced by the books' appearances on the show. The respondents answered two simple questions, illustrated in Figures 1 and 2, and then provided some insightful feedback about their reading habits. They also listed their favorite "*Lost* books," which I used to compile a "Top Ten" list of the most popular books among viewers. I posed this question in the title of the survey: "Has *Lost* inspired you to read?"

One fan reported that he "recently started reading *The Stand*, dug out my old *Of Mice and Men*, and last week purchased *Valis* and *Slaughterhouse-Five*. Oh, and hadn't read a book in about five years before *Lost* and now I can't stop. So you could say it has inspired me to read" (Stuart, Has 'Lost' Inspired You to Read? 2010). Another viewer claimed that, "[*Lost*] inspired me to finish writing one I started some 20 years ago." One DocArzt fan expressed his desire to commit some time to reading all of the *Lost* books: "I read *Watership Down* and one of the short stories in Flannery O'Conner's collection. I'm planning to do a serious read of *Lost*-referenced books after the series is over, including *The Dark Tower* series.

It seems that fans have created a space for renewed discussion of classic works of literature among mostly casual readers. Many fan sites, including "The Fuselage" and "DarkUFO" have separate forums for discussing the literary allusions and several blogs, like *The Lost Books Challenge* are created for the sole reason of sharing the reading experience with others, as well as the viewing experience (*Lost Books Challenge* 2009).

In some cases the series has inspired those who self-identify as non-readers to begin reading again. The following comments illustrate a trend that I observed within the *Lost* fan base: the community of fans interested in the metanarrative has been extended into book clubs, making the viewers' central purpose the discussion of serious literary works. Not only did they become interested in new books because of the series, but they leave the discussion of *Lost* completely and approach the books outside the context of the show, initiating a discourse and opening a new space for a community of readers. The following set of comments posted on the DocArzt fan site demonstrates the course of development leading into an evaluative discussion of literature:

"DeSelby":   [*The Brothers Karamazov*] is amazing, and
                  deals with patricide, which is appropriate
                  given that we saw Ben reading it and
                  discussing it with Locke. I tried to read
                  Ulysses a few times before it was on *Lost* but
                  never made it far. I read *The Third Policeman*
                  after it was in the hatch and loved it . . . which
                  I'm sure is obvious to anyone familiar with
                  that book.

"The Magician":   I want to start on *The Brothers Karamazov*
                  at some point, although I'm not really into
                  Dostoyevsky — I tried to read *Crime &*
                  Punishment a few years ago and found myself
                  giving up after 50 or so pages.

"DeSelby":   I'd still try it. It's long but has a lot of short
                  stories within to break it up. A friend of mine
                  and I both read *The Brothers Karamozov* at
                  around the same time and both loved it, then
                  we both tried *Crime & Punishment* and got
                  only about as far as you did.

"Cajuncook":   Funny, but I was the opposite. I thought
                  C&P was a masterpiece; definitely one of my
                  favorite books ever written. [*The*] *Brothers*
                  Karamazov was a masterpiece to me, too,
                  but in a very different way that made it so
                  difficult to read as a novel. It was terrific to
                  analyze in an academic sense, but so freaking
                  difficult to read page by page for joy.
                  (Stuart, "Has 'Lost' Inspired You to Read?" 2010)

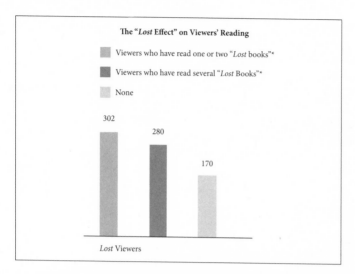

Figure 1 Viewers' responses to the following question: "Have you ever read or re-read any of the books featured or referenced in *Lost*, in response to their appearance on the show?"

Source: Stuart, *Books and Lost* 2010

*Specifically in response to the program.

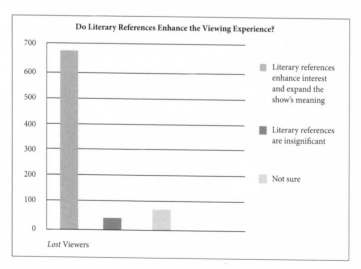

Figure 2 Viewers' response to the survey question: "Do the literary references enhance your experience as a viewer of Lost?"

Source: Stuart, *Books and Lost* 2010

The survey results, illustrated in Figures 1 and 2, align with the anecdotal comments posted on both the survey site and the DocArzt website. The numbers show a strong relationship between fans viewing *Lost* and reading its book "suggestions." Out of the 752 respondents, 582 have read at least one of the books referenced on the show, in response to an episode appearance (Figure 1). Figure 2 reflects the significance that viewers perceive the book references to have. More than 650 viewers reported that the books enhanced their interest in *Lost* and expanded the meaning of the series (Stuart, *Books and Lost* 2010).

Top Ten Most Popular Books Among *Lost* Viewers

(The following books are also based on data from the survey, but not listed in a particular order.)

1. *Slaughterhouse-Five*, Kurt Vonnegut
2. *Alice's Adventures in Wonderland* and *Through the Looking-Glass and What Alice Found There*, Lewis Carroll
3. *The Stand*, Stephen King
4. *Everything That Rises Must Converge*, Flannery O'Connor
5. *Our Mutual Friend*, Charles Dickens
6. *The Turn of the Screw*, Henry James
7. *Watership Down*, Richard Adams
8. *Of Mice and Men*, John Steinbeck
9. *The Brothers Karamazov*, Fyodor Dostoevsky
10. *The Third Policeman*, Flann O'Brien

The results of this survey reveal that a majority of viewers are responsive to the explicit and implicit literary references presented in *Lost*. In order to take a more active role in the narrative, fans engage in reading experiences that might take a considerable amount of time and effort away from the viewing experience. *Lost* heightens their awareness of other texts, works of fiction that may have escaped their attention prior to the show, but have taken on new meaning in light of the series. I have heard much anecdotal evidence to support this claim, but this is the first large set of data that reveals the strong correlation between viewers of *Lost* and newly inspired readers. The next section provides a snapshot of this connection, in relation to one particular book cameo.

The legend of *The Third Policeman*

Chad Post was serving as editor of the Dalkey Archive Press when Flann O'Brien's *The Third Policeman*, a Dalkey Press book, appeared in the season-two episode, "Man of Science, Man of Faith." Although some books appeared in the first season, Post thinks that his press was the first to really benefit from the exposure that *Lost* provided. His press sold as many copies in the three weeks following the book's *Lost* placement, as it had in the six years prior to the episode. That translates to 15,000 copies in less than a month. The book, and other works by O'Brien, continued to sell at high rates continuing into the next summer, when Post moved to another press, no longer having access to Dalkey's sales (Post, Interview 2010). Fueling the fire of the jump in sales were Craig Wright's comments published in the *Chicago Tribune* on September 21, 2005, and cited in the online source, *Lostpedia*. He is quoted as saying "whoever goes out and buys the book will have a lot more ammunition in their back pocket when theorizing about the show . . . and, no small thing, they will have read a really great book" ("The Third Policeman," *Lostpedia* 2005).

Lost writer Gregg Nations first contacted Post in 2005 to obtain permission to use *The Third Policeman* on the show. The two discussed other possibilities for featured novels and from that point forward, Post acted as an unofficial book consultant. *The Invention of Morel*, which appeared in season five's "La Fleur," was one of Post's suggestions, but generally the writing team would propose a book and Post simply advised. They often asked him about themes, looking for books that might address the overarching ideas of the show (Post, Interview 2010).

The Crying of Lot 49 was never featured, but it is one that both Nations and Post agree resonate with the style and story line of the show. When Post suggested the Thomas Pynchon book, Nations had already been considering it: "we've always wanted to use it," he told Post. In an article posted on *The Wall Street Journal*'s *Speakeasy* blog, Post says "I hope the final moments of *Lost* echo the ambiguously abrupt ending of *The Crying of Lot 49*, which leaves the reader tantalizingly close to resolution but forces them to go back through the book time and again, revisiting key brilliant passages in hopes of figuring it all out" (Post, "*Lost* Premiere" 2010) Another of Post's favorites, a book that was featured twice, is Philip K. Dick's *VALIS*. He thinks that this novel reveals the nature of *Lost*; it is about "belief and how the characters interpret what's happening" versus what might really be happening. The story line is convincing but subject to scrutiny; the events are channeled through a mentally unstable character, an unreliable narrator.

Regarding the question of *Lost*'s enduring narrative value, Post describes *Lost* as having a nineteenth-century Dickensian and Dostoevskian storytelling quality, but is also characterized by its postmodern ambiguity and "other-worldly" flavor of Flannery O'Connor. He points out that the writers of *Lost* use literary devices effectively, such as motifs, catch phrases, allegory and non-linear storytelling. "They do a fine job of crafting a good story within the constraints of being a mass market franchise . . . [*Lost* has] revolutionized the way TV functions in our society" (Post, Interview 2010) To extend this evaluation of *Lost*, I offer Ivan Askwith's claim that the series is the most "novelistic show on US broadcast television." Askwith explains that "each episode of the series functions not as an independent narrative unit but as a sequential link in a chain that stretches from the first episode to the last, framing the entire series as a single narrative, rather than an overlapping series of related narratives" (Askwith 2009).

Based on Post's suggestions and the Dalkey Archive Press phenomenon, a side-effect of viewers' literary interest in the show is made clear: there was a turning point in the types of books placed after *The Third Policeman*, as well as the writers' awareness of the audience's attention to book "props." Once it became clear that viewers were paying greater attention, the producers began to take the literary references more seriously. The astute response of the viewers resulted in a more careful approach to literary allusion.

Organization of this book

Literary Lost is organized thematically. Each chapter, with the exception of the first, focuses on one pervasive idea from the series, using several central texts to support the implications of that theme in *Lost*. Chapter 1 is a complete reference of the books featured on the show or that have an implied connection to the show. Chapter 2 explores the notion and value of faith in a higher power, using comparison texts that include works by Flannery O'Connor, C. S. Lewis and Soren Kierkegaard. Chapter 3 focuses on a question central to meaning-making in *Lost*: Do human beings have free will or are their lives predetermined? Chapter 4 addresses *Lost*'s generic identity and explores time travel as a storytelling device. Chapter 5 addresses how *Lost* identifies the relationship between parent and child and dramatizes the family unit, with Fyodor Dostoevsky's *The Brothers Karamazov* presented as a key text. Chapter 6 delves into the psychological implications of dreams, visions and hallucinations in *Lost*, examining how the line between illusions and the supernatural is blurred. Chapter 7 positions the characters' group dynamics in a literary context by exploring works such as *Lord of the Flies* and *Lost Horizon*, castaway stories in which small groups are challenged to work together in order to survive. The conclusion in Chapter 8 provides a broader perspective of the purpose of fictional narratives and the potential that television might have as a medium that can both "delight and instruct."

Literary Lost suggests that *Lost* offers viewers an opportunity to extend their experience through books. It reveals a book club quality, offering a deeper understanding of the texts at hand, but tapping into questions and issues that require further contemplation and dialogue with others. It seeks to extend the discussion of *Lost's* literature beyond the websites and online forums that operate around the hype of each new episode. This book is designed for viewers who want to know more about the significance of the show's chosen texts, but it also remains accessible to readers unfamiliar with the television series. In either case, readers who are interested in exploring how popular texts from one medium have the potential to revitalize the discussion of texts from another, might find a point of initiation in this book.

1

The Books of *Lost*

This chapter contains more than 90 literary works relevant to seasons one through six of *Lost*. These books have enjoyed on-screen appearances, direct allusions and/or implied references to the series. Some demonstrate a strong link to the show, while others are associated simply through a shared theme or narrative device. Presented in the first section are the books pertinent to more than one season. The middle section provides a catalogue of the rest of the books, organized by season, and the final section includes works that are less obvious as "*Lost* texts."

This extensive listing can serve as a reference tool for the subsequent chapters of this book, which offer thematic explorations of selected works. For each entry below, a brief description is provided, as well as an explanation of its relevance to the series. The more thorough descriptions usually indicate a greater significance to *Lost* (and to this book) but the summaries vary greatly in length. Some of these texts are fictitious and exist only within the diegesis of the show. Other books may seem to have little in common with the show's themes but are still included here, if only to demonstrate the large volume of the show's allusions. For instance, *Memoirs of a Geisha* and *Are You There God, It's Me, Margaret* have little or no bearing on the storyline of *Lost* but are incorporated here simply because of their prominent screen time.

Note: The selected texts mentioned in subsequent chapters are designated with an asterisk (*).

Books associated with more than one season

*Alice's Adventures in Wonderland,** Lewis Carroll

The writers of *Lost* pay homage to both *Alice's Adventures in Wonderland* and *Through the Looking-Glass and What Alice Found There*, evidence of which can be found in episode titles ("White Rabbit," "Through the Looking Glass"), themes (altered identity, transformation and growth), and overtly comparable images (more than one character either falls or climbs down a "rabbit hole").

In the first Alice story, the young heroine follows a white rabbit to an alternate reality where commonly held notions of the material world do not apply. Animals can speak, a baby turns into a pig, playing cards have human features and "everyone is mad," according to one Cheshire cat. The adventure is presumably a dream sequence, a notion that the reader discovers in the final chapter when Alice is awakened by her sister. *Alice's Adventures in Wonderland* is the story of a child struggling to understand the harsh reality of the adult world and working through those problems in a fantasy life. The predicaments Alice faces in Wonderland are exaggerated reflections of the real world.

In the same way, the characters of *Lost* work through their pre-crash issues in mythic proportions on the island, whether by hunting for boar or running from monsters. The island is a Wonderland where the original inhabitants are both mysterious and hostile. Word games, number puzzles, moving backwards in time, changing identity, and the notion of sanity are common to both Carroll's narrative and *Lost*. The white rabbit, and rabbits in general, are a recurring image in *Lost* — they signify the threshold to another world, as demonstrated by their important role in time-travel experiments. Viewers will also recall the prominently featured white rabbits in season six just prior to Desmond's passage through an electromagnetic portal to the ultimate "wonderland" — the afterlife — and back again ("Happily Ever After").

For a description of the other Alice story see "Through the Looking Glass and What Alice Found There" listed under season three.

Biblical texts*

The sacred narratives of Christian-Judeo origin permeate the mythology of *Lost* to such an extent that some of the story's meaning would be unrealized without the connections to these texts. The writers attach biblical significance to the series in various ways. One of the more obvious approaches is the naming of episode titles after (biblical) book titles or passages: "Numbers," "Exodus," "The 23rd Psalm" and "316" and "Fire + Water." Another device used to convey religious meaning is the actual appearance of the Bible on screen. Boone sees a bible in the crashed Beechcraft, Desmond is shown with one in the hatch, Eko finds one in the Arrow Station and later shows it to Locke, and, in a flashback, Eko finds Yemi's King James version in the church. There is also quotation: on two occasions Eko quotes Psalm 23 (if incorrectly) and engraves several other passages on his walking stick. A final key source of biblical allusion is the naming of characters. Aaron, Jacob, Ben, John, James, Isaac, Sarah, Adam, and Thomas (Tom) are names found in the Bible, primarily in the Old Testament. Notable too, is the name Christian Shephard, a clear reference to Jesus, a figure characterized in Christianity as a shepherd of humanity.

A Christmas Carol, Charles Dickens

Sawyer refers to the Smoke Monster (Locke) as the Ghost of Christmas Past, one of the three spirits that visit Ebenezer Scrooge in this classic Dickens story about the dramatic transformation of a miserly Briton living in nineteenth-century London ("The Substitute").

Sawyer calls himself "The Ghost of Christmas Future" in season five when banging on Desmond's door to the hatch ("Because You Left").

The Chronicles of Narnia,* C. S. Lewis

This popular Christian series by C. S. (Clive Staples) Lewis, first published in 1950, tells the story of a hidden universe that can be accessed only by the chosen. The supernatural land of Narnia is populated by mystical creatures, most of them talking animals, including Aslan the lion, unambiguously represented as a Christ figure. The protagonists, four siblings, first cross into Narnia through a portal in an enchanted wardrobe. They become involved in a war, a struggle between good and evil, a manifestation of personal spiritual warfare. The allegorical series involves a sacrificial, god-like figure (Aslan) and forces of the devil, embodied by the White Witch and her constituents.

In the first book, *The Lion, the Witch and the Wardrobe*, a lamppost marks the threshold between Narnia and the real world, similar to the way in which the Lamp Post station in Los Angeles serves as a bridge to the island world. Sacrifice and resurrection, familiar motifs in *Lost*, play a key role in this story.

The naming of Charlotte Staples Lewis, *Lost*'s anthropologist sent to the island as part of a team of specialists, is a nod to Lewis and his works.

Heart of Darkness,* Joseph Conrad

Although he is unseen through much of the story, Kurtz is the central figure of this famous work by Joseph Conrad. The mystery of *Heart of Darkness* is not so much the "savagery" of the jungle but, rather, the identity of Kurtz. Marlow, the internal narrator, is on a quest to understand the true nature of this man, and of men in general. Are they inherently evil? Are all men as easily corruptible as Kurtz?

Marlow, a sailor working for a Belgian trading company, is responsible for retrieving Mr. Kurtz from the "Inner Station" deep within the Congo. He has heard many good things about the man — that he is talented, successful in the ivory trade and a great leader of men. From others he hears that Kurtz is a gentleman and great humanitarian. But when Marlow and his crew finally find the Inner Station, they find a very different man. Marlow discovers Kurtz in a wretched condition, extremely ill and half insane. "I saw the inconceivable mystery of a soul that knew no restraint, no faith and no fear, yet struggling blindly with itself" (Conrad 1995, 386). He learns that Kurtz is acting as a warlord over the natives and forcing them to work under the most unbearable conditions. His own village worships him as a supernatural being and he raids the surrounding communities, pillaging for ivory and then claiming it as his own. As evidenced by the human heads mounted on stakes, Marlow can clearly see how Kurtz operates his ivory business.

Marlow and his team manage to load the sick man onto the steamboat, but Kurtz dies before they arrive home. His dying words, "the horror, the horror," were used in a promotional trailer for episode 6.14, "The Candidate," along with another line from the story, slightly altered: "But his soul was mad. Being alone in the wilderness."

In season one Jack asks Kate, "Tell me something, how come every time there's a hike into the heart of darkness you sign up?"

Charlie refers to Hurley as "Colonel bloody Kurtz" ("Numbers") and Sawyer nicknames John "Colonel Kurtz" in "Confirmed Dead."[1]

According to *Lostpedia*, "in the non-canonical *Lost: Via Domus*, a copy of *Heart of Darkness* can be found in a set of caves inhabited by polar bears."

Lord of the Flies,* William Golding

This survival tale about a group of English schoolboys who crash on an island is a clear model for the series, although Golding's obvious pessimism about human nature is not matched in *Lost*. In the novel, no adults are among the survivors of the plane crash and the boys are forced to govern themselves. They begin to develop a community but it quickly disintegrates into chaotic savagery. See Chapter 7 for a detailed examination of this novel's themes.

Sawyer tells Jack that "it's *Lord of the Flies* time now" when justifying his looting practices ("In Translation").

Charlie explains that the survivors from the tail end of the plane went "all *Lord of the Flies*" to indicate their deterioration of civility compared to the relatively well-ordered society still intact in the primary set of castaways ("What Kate Did").

Moby Dick, Herman Melville

Considered one of the great American novels, *Moby Dick* tells the story of Captain Ahab, a sea captain who seeks revenge on the whale that purportedly destroyed his ship and bit off his leg. The connection to *Lost* is a tenuous one (Sawyer nicknames Sayid "Captain A-rab" in "Three Minutes"), although any man-versus-nature, seafaring adventure seems a good comparison text to the show. Sawyer alludes to the book again in season six: "Thar she blows," he says in reference to *The Elizabeth*, the sailboat intended to serve as a mode of escape in "The Last Recruit."

Of Mice and Men,* John Steinbeck

This short novel tells the story of a deep friendship between two migrant workers near California's Soledad River in the 1930s. George acts as caretaker of Lenny, a grown man with a very low IQ. They are compelled to move from job to job and farm to farm because of Lenny's unintentional destructive acts. The tragic ending underscores the novel's themes of isolation, loneliness and compassion.

The writers of *Lost* have gestured toward this work more than once over the course of the series. In season six Sawyer tells John (the Smoke Monster) that it is his favorite book, a good choice for a loner who has just lost the one true love of his life. Sawyer is similar to George — they both are world-weary and hardened, but deeply compassionate and vulnerable at times.

The other exchange that calls attention to *Of Mice and Men* takes place between Sawyer and Ben in "Every Man for Himself" when Sawyer wants to know if Ben is taking him to "That little place you always wanted, George?" Later, Ben quotes the book too: "A guy goes nuts if he ain't got nobody. It don't make any difference who the guy is, so long as he's with you. I tell ya . . . I tell ya, a guy gets too lonely, and he gets sick." Sawyer is shown reading *Of Mice and Men* in the same episode.

Our Mutual Friend, Charles Dickens

This complex tale deals with fate, coincidence and human interdependence, all noteworthy themes in *Lost*. The Thames River figures significantly in the plot of *Our Mutual Friend*, just as the ocean and water are symbols of mystery, power and death in *Lost*.

One of the more explicit literary references, this Penguin English Library edition gets a good bit of screen time. It is the last novel that Desmond plans to read before he dies (an idea the writers of *Lost* borrowed from the legend that John Irving is saving *Our Mutual Friend* for his last read (Lindelof, *The Lost Book Club* 2007)). The book also serves as a hiding place for the failsafe key and where Penny tucks a letter of encouragement for Desmond's deepest moment of despair.

Penny and Desmond's boat is named *Our Mutual Friend*. When Ben spots Penny on her boat, with the intention of killing her, he tells Charles Widmore (over the phone), "I'm looking at our mutual friend right now" ("Dead is Dead"). In a subsequent scene Ben shoots Desmond and Desmond attacks Ben, pushing him into the water, bloody and beaten. Although Ben survives, this image recalls the body that is at the center of the novel's mystery, a dead man who has been dredged out of the Thames.

Robinson Crusoe, Daniel Defoe

The original island survival novel, Defoe's work set a precedent for hundreds of subsequent shipwreck tales. In 1719, when the *Life and Strange Surprising Adventures of Robinson Crusoe* (its original title) was first published, the danger of finding unnavigated waters and unknown lands was still very real for the colonizing Western world. The idea of a young gentleman alone on an island was a terrifying notion.

Unlike the characters on *Lost*, Crusoe initially finds himself completely alone. Every man among his crew has died and he must scavenge among the shipwreck for food and for materials to make a shelter. But the similarities to *Lost* are apparent too: eventually Crusoe encounters "Others," natives of the island; like Michael, he builds a boat; and like many of the series' characters, he develops a newfound spiritual life while awaiting rescue.

The Stand, Stephen King

The executive producers of *Lost*, Carlton Cuse and Damon Lindelof, have claimed that this epic novel, first published in 1978, has strongly influenced the show's premise. According to Cuse, "King's *The Stand* was a blueprint for the show because it was this very long, character-oriented book that hung on a high-concept premise that the entire nation had been infected with this super-flu, and it was the equivalent of people crashing on this mysterious island. Both based on incredibly intricate and involved character dynamics" (Bradner 2009).

This text and its association to *Lost* has already been addressed to a good extent in other publications. For example, in *Lost's Buried Treasures*, Lynette Porter, David Lavery and Hillary Robson provide a thorough comparison of the book and the show.

*Watership Down,** Richard Adams

Well known by fans as Sawyer's "book about bunnies," *Watership Down* illustrates social conflict and human nature through the lives of wild rabbit communities.

Prompted by his own prophetic vision, Fiver warns the others that they must abandon their comfortable warren to avoid an impending catastrophe. His brother, Hazel, becomes the reluctant leader, similar in nature to Jack Shephard's characterization. They embark on a journey into an uncertain future, experiencing all of the struggles that come with the re-establishment of society after the social order has been upended. Together they face natural predators, harsh conditions and conflicts with other warrens, as they struggle to survive the challenges of life without the security of an established civilization.

The book can be seen in "Confidence Man" in Boone's posses-sion. In the same episode Sawyer is seen reading it; he also reads it in "Left Behind." In "Recon" (season six), it is featured once again when Charlotte is rummaging through Sawyer's dresser in a flash sideways scene.

*The Wonderful Wizard of Oz,** L. Frank Baum

It seems that the writers of *Lost* are relying on the viewers' knowledge of the film version of this classic story rather than the original children's novel by L. Frank Baum. *The Wizard of Oz*, as the movie is titled, is so entrenched in American pop culture that its reference can always serve as a reliable storytelling tool. However, I will allude to the written work here, with the acknowledgment that the film is the better known of the two.

The Wonderful Wizard of Oz, originally published in 1900, tells the story of a Kansas farm girl and her journey through the strange land of Oz, an alternate universe of sorts, and her quest to find a way back home. Along the way she meets a scarecrow, a tin woodman and a lion. Each companion is on his own quest to find something he is missing, each a significant component of a complete person — intelligence, love and courage. Like the characters in *Lost* they are relying on someone else (the wizard and Glinda) to make up for their sense of emptiness.

A Wrinkle in Time, Madeleine L'Engle

Meg is the central heroine in this young adult fantasy novel in which three children embark on a quest to rescue the girl's father, a time-traveling scientist. He has been captured by a malevolent entity (IT) which is under the spell of "The Black Thing," a force described as a dark cloud. In order to move quickly through space and time, the characters use a "wrinkle," where the fabric of the universe is folded together. The children find him on Camazotz, a mind-controlling planet where all of the inhabitants are hypnotized by IT. Eventually they overcome this dark force on Camazotz, but it is made clear that the "Black Thing" cannot be entirely defeated, only controlled. This dark cloud is similar to the smoke monster of *Lost* that is kept in check by a cork-like wedge that keeps the evil contained but never fully eradicated.

Sawyer is seen reading this fantasy novel in "Numbers." It is featured again in "Recon" (season six) when Charlotte is rummaging through Sawyer's dresser in a flash sideways scene.

Season one books

Memoirs of a Geisha, Arthur Golden

A fictional account of Japanese culture seen through the eyes of a successful geisha, this story is referenced in "Exodus, Part 1" when Jin shows his irritation toward Sun in a public place (the airport), after she spills coffee on his lap. An English-speaking onlooker comments on their relationship, assuming Sun does not understand English.

Season two books

Beyond Freedom and Dignity,* B. F. Skinner

A controversial figure in the field of psychology, B. F. Skinner proposed that rather than relying on old notions of free will and autonomy, psychologists should explore more scientific methods to manipulate human behavior.

The Dharma Initiative's interest in behaviorism, as revealed in their experiments implemented in the various stations and the cages, demonstrates a reflection of the tenets proposed in this nonfiction text. But there is also a direct reference to the author in the orientation film: Dr. Marvin Candle presents a history of the Dharma Initiative, describing the founders as "following in the footsteps of visionaries such as B. F. Skinner" ("What Kate Did").

After All These Years, Susan Isaacs

This mystery novel, published in 1994, tells the story of a New Jersey English teacher falsely accused of killing her estranged husband with a knife from her own kitchen. The heroine must find the true killer in order to prove her innocence. In the meantime she unearths evidence of her dead husband's secret life.

The book can be seen in the Swan station next to the bed where Sawyer is recovering from the raft incident ("Everybody Hates Hugo"). Few significant shared themes are apparent between *Lost* and *After All These Years* and many fans have speculated that this novel is merely a prop, not intended to add meaning to the series.

Are You There God? It's Me, Margaret, Judy Blume

This young adult novel tells the story of Margaret, an adolescent girl dealing with issues of spirituality and the inevitable physical changes of puberty. As she struggles to find her place in the world, she turns to organized religion for the answers to some of life's bigger questions.

It is given a bit of screen time in "The Whole Truth," and elicits a colorful line from Sawyer as he sits in his signature devil-may-care reading pose on the beach. When Sun asks him about the book he replies, "Predictable . . . not nearly enough sex."

Bad Twin, Gary Troup

Fictional author Gary Troup was a passenger on *Lost*'s flight, Oceanic 815. He survived the crash but died when he was sucked into the jet fan. Hyperion Books published this novel under the character's name.

The manuscript of this novel is seen in "The Long Con" and "Two for the Road."

Bluebeard, Charles Perrault's version

When this story begins, the extremely wealthy Bluebeard has already been married several times, but each wife mysteriously disappeared shortly after her wedding. Now he is looking for a new bride, but his blue beard is considered to be hideous and frightening to everyone, especially women. Despite this, he eventually convinces a neighbor to marry him. Shortly after the wedding, his new wife discovers a small room filled with the corpses of Bluebeard's previous wives. The husband threatens to behead her for discovering this room, but, before he can carry out the murder, the young woman's brothers arrive and kill Bluebeard.

Several versions of this story have been recorded, but here I will assume that the brief allusion, one of Sawyer's nicknames in *Lost*, refers to Charles Perrault's folk tale written in 1697. In "Adrift," Michael and Sawyer argue about the Others' attack on their boat and the kidnapping of Walt. Sawyer refers to Tom, the bearded leader of the Others' boat crew, in the following line of dialogue: "Hell, Bluebeard blew us up because he wanted your kid." Indeed, this Other, later to be revealed as a sophisticated agent of Ben's cause, continuously maintains an aura of dangerous power, much like the monstrous

Bluebeard. Tom Friendly and crew, like Bluebeard, are responsible for a multitude of deaths and even have a stash of corpses hidden away (the murdered Dharma Initiative employees seen in "The Man Behind the Curtain").

The Book of Law

In "What Kate Did" Locke views part of the "Orientation" videotape. He and Eko are in the kitchen area of the underground bunker when Eko tells Locke the following biblical story:

> At that time the temple where the people worshipped was in ruin. And so the people worshipped idols, false gods. And so the kingdom was in disarray. Josiah, since he was a good king, sent his secretary to the treasury and said, "We must rebuild the temple. Give all of the gold to the workers so that this will be done." But when the secretary returned, he had no gold. And when Josiah asked why this was the secretary replied, "We found a book." . . . What the secretary had found was an ancient book, the Book of Law. You may know it as the Old Testament. And it was with that ancient book, not with the gold, that Josiah rebuilt the temple. On the other side of the island we found a place much like this, and in this place we found a book.

Eko reveals a book and pushes it toward Locke saying, "I believe what's inside there will be of great value to you." This story is recorded in both the second book of Kings and the second book of Chronicles in the Old Testament. It is a tale of reconciliation with the "one true God" and a return to monotheism. After reading this "Book of Law," King Josiah tells his high priests and scribes that "the anger of the Lord has been set furiously ablaze against us, because our fathers did not obey the stipulations of this book" (2 Kgs 22.13, NASB).

Another Book of Law turns up again in "Cabin Fever" when Richard Alpert asks a young John Locke to choose among three items one thing that belongs to him. One item is a book of considerable age and wear, titled *Book of Laws*. John does not choose the book, but a knife instead.

*The Brothers Karamazov,** Fyodor Dostoevsky

Fyodor Karamazov is the crude but wealthy patriarch of a messy family situation. His four sons Dmitri, Ivan, Alyosha and the illegitimate Smerdyakov all harbor varying degrees of bitterness toward their father whose murder becomes the center of the drama. Dmitri is charged for the crime, while Ivan feels somewhat responsible and Smerdyakov bears the actual guilt. Amid all of this, Alyosha, the most virtuous of the family, is devastated, not only by the death of his father, but by the behavior of his brothers.

Each brother seems to characterize a broad archetype: Dmitri is the sensual one, Ivan is the intellectual and Alyosha is the spiritual brother. Smerdyakov, the downtrodden, illegitimate son, is consumed by resentment. *The Brothers Karamazov* is an especially good example of intertextuality in the sphere of *Lost* literature. A character in Kurt Vonnegut's *Slaughterhouse-Five* claims that this Russian novel contains "everything there was to know about life" (Vonnegut, 129). *The Brothers Karamazov* appears more than an entire season before Desmond utters the words "unstuck in time," a phrase borrowed from Vonnegut's 1969 cult novel, but the connection is there, not only in this circle of references, but also because of thematic similarities. *The Brothers Karamazov* is a story about redemption through suffering, but also about free will, faith, parricide and the question of immortality. In a characteristically postmodern manner, the series points to one text which, in turn, points to the other, creating a chain of narratives that compels each text to emerge in a new light.

Dostoevsky's style is similar to *Lost* in that it engages many perspectives, not one of them having exclusive authority. This polyphonic quality of Dostoevsky's work was mastered in his final epic work, *The Brothers Karamazov*. Considering novels are, by nature, individualistic and solitary, conveying Bakhtin's concept of the "carnival" of a community was no small task. A long-running television series lends itself more easily to this style because of fluid shifts in perspective, the ability to portray large groups of people at once and the length of time necessary to construct a polyphonic voice.

The Brothers Karamazov appears on screen in "Maternity Leave" when Henry Gale (also known as Benjamin Linus) is held captive in a vault at the Swan station. Locke offers him some reading material in the form of this novel, Dostoevsky's last and greatest work. Later in the same episode, Henry/Ben draws a map to Henry Gale's balloon on the back of this novel's title page.

The Epic of Gilgamesh

In "Collision," Eko completes a crossword puzzle (42 down) using the word Gilgamesh, the title of a Babylonian epic poem dating as early as the third millennium BC, and the name of the story's central character. The poem is reputed to be the earliest written text ever found.

Gilgamesh, a Babylonian king, befriends Enkidu, a wild animal-like man who initially tries to kill him. Once they overcome their differences, the two men form a deep bond as they embark on a journey together to kill Humbaba, lord of the cedar forest who poses a threat to them both. They succeed, but then face a conflict with the gods, resulting in Enkidu's death. Grief-stricken at the death of his friend, Gilgamesh pledges to find a way to bring him back, even venturing to the land of the dead to restore Enkidu's life. This last part of the story is something of a spiritual mystery, similar to the religious puzzle pieces of *Lost*.

The friendship of Gilgamesh and Enkidu has been compared by many fans and critics to that of Eko and Locke. But in light of season five, the more obvious comparison is to Jack and John. Although they were not so much friends as rivals, theirs was a deep connection of which Jack felt the full impact upon John's death. This is when he dedicates his whole life to returning to the island where John is, in a sense, raised from the dead.

High Hand, Gary Phillips

The first installment of the Martha Chainey Mysteries series, this 2001 novel chronicling ex-showgirl Martha Chainey's misadventures working for the Las Vegas mob is seen on the Swan station bookshelf in "Orientation."

Hindsight, Peter Wright

Sawyer is reading this self-published, science-fiction novel while recovering in the hatch in "Everybody Hates Hugo." It is about a device that will allow present-day viewers to observe events from the past. Two scientific researchers, funded by a wealthy benefactor, create a contraption not to travel through time, but as a means to view the past — hence, the title. This idea is similar to the fictional device created by Adolfo Bioy Casares (see *The Invention of Morel*, listed here).

Julius Caesar, William Shakespeare

There are two explicit allusions to this dramatic work: Sawyer says, "You too, Brutus?" to Locke in "Two for the Road." The other reference is season five's character, Caesar, whose short-lived appearance ends in a gunshot to the chest, courtesy of Ben Linus.

Lancelot, Walker Percy

A man named Lancelot is committed to an insane asylum after killing his wife for an adulterous act that resulted in the birth of "their" youngest child. The novel explores the nature of betrayal, specifically adultery, and its effects on the injured party. The narrative takes the form of Lancelot's memories, or flashbacks, while he is confined in the institution.

Sawyer is reading this fictional work on the beach in "Maternity Leave."

Kate Austen kills her father/stepfather, Wayne, in the same way Lancelot kills his wife, by setting off an explosion in the house. Her mother led Kate to believe that Wayne was not her real father.

The question of paternity also hangs over Sun's pregnancy.

The novel is featured again in "Recon" (season six) when Charlotte is rummaging through Sawyer's dresser in a flash sideways scene.

"An Occurrence at Owl Creek Bridge,"* Ambrose Bierce

The structure of this short story has been noted for its similarities to *Lost*'s flashback/flashforward storytelling. A man is hanged at Owl Creek Bridge. The rope snaps and the man escapes and travels by foot to his home, all the way experiencing a painful sensation in his neck. When he finally arrives at his gate, he approaches his wife and tries to embrace her, but suddenly feels a "stunning blow upon the back of the neck . . . then all is darkness and silence" (Bierce 1970, 53). The soldier is dead with a broken neck, still hanging above Owl Creek. The entire journey of returning home is a hallucination and the entire narrative is, in a sense, "just a dream." This is similar to the slow forward movement of the narrative in *Lost*. The memories and dreams of the characters change the pace of the present action.

Bierce himself has been the object of mysterious circumstances and speculation. He disappeared without a trace in January 1914 when he crossed the border into Mexico intending to join the forces of Pancho Villa. He was 72 years old at the time and was never seen again. Bierce wrote a multitude of short stories with nautical themes and mysterious endings including "A Psychological Shipwreck" and "The Damned Thing," both noted in *Lost's Buried Treasures* as relevant to *Lost* (Porter et al. 2007).

Bierce appears as a character in the novella, *Lost Legacy*, by Robert Heinlein, another "*Lost* author" listed here (see *Stranger in a Strange Land* and "By His Bootstraps"),

In "The Long Con" John can be seen rifling through the pages of this collection of short stories in the Swan station.

The Outsiders, S. E. Hinton

This novel, originally published in 1967, illustrates the division between the "insiders" and the "outsiders" of a small town in Tulsa, Oklahoma, specifically as it affects the politics of high school society. The plot centers on Ponyboy and Johnny, two "Greasers" (outsiders).

In a flashback from "Everybody Hates Hugo," Johnny uses this popular novel's famous quote, "Stay gold, Ponyboy," to encourage Hurley to stay strong and be true to himself. The quote refers to a poem by Robert Frost, "Nothing Gold Can Stay."

The Pearl, John Steinbeck

An impoverished diver finds a beautiful pearl that initially holds a promise of new hope, but it becomes a symbol of greed and corruption.

In *Lost*, "The Pearl" is the name of a Dharma station, a small hatch used mainly for surveillance. It is first discovered in season one when Nikki and Paolo stumble across it, but in season two it has more screen time after Eko finds it.

Rainbow Six, Tom Clancy

Secret agent John Clark is charged with battling a group of terrorists who are intent on eradicating humanity by means of biological warfare.

In "Orientation" this book is seen on the bookshelf.

*The Third Policeman,** Flann O'Brien (also known as Brian O'Nolan or Brian O'Nuallian)

The unnamed narrator in this postmodern novel is caught in a torturous and confusing recurring loop of hell after his involvement in a theft and a murder. See Chapter 3 for a detailed examination of the narrative and its connection to *Lost*.

This book has often been cited as an example of viewers responding to a featured work of literature on *Lost*. See the introduction for details about this phenomenon from the perspective of the novel's publisher, the Dalkey Archive Press.

In "Man of Science, Man of Faith" the book can be seen on Desmond's bunk. He appears to be reading it when the survivors of the plane crash enter the hatch for the first time.

*The Turn of the Screw,** Henry James

A governess struggles to protect her two charges from malevolent apparitions that haunt the countryside estate in Victorian England. However, it quickly becomes apparent to the discerning reader that this young woman might be mentally unstable and the "ghosts" just hallucinations. Henry James was known as a master of ambiguity and unreliable narrators. In the same vein, *Lost* keeps viewers guessing the intentions and motives of each character, questioning the lens of his or her flashbacks.

One of the two children in the mistress's charge is a boy named Miles. He seems to be able to see one of the ghosts but, this too, is open to interpretation. Similarly, *Lost*'s Miles Straum communicates with ghosts, especially the newly deceased, to determine the causes of their deaths.

The Swan Orientation film is hidden behind this book, as seen in "Orientation."

Season three books

Animal Farm, George Orwell

Orwell's political satire dramatizes a movement of social unrest represented by farm animals and their human oppressors. A revolution arises at Manor Farm when the animals drive out the farmers. Led by the pigs, the animals take control of the farm and establish their own community, governed by the Seven Commandments of Animalism. The first law states that "whatever goes upon two legs is an enemy." (See a more detailed summary of *Animal Farm* in Chapter 7.)

In his frustration at the self-ordained group of leaders (Jack, Kate and John), Leslie Arzt utters an explicit reference to George Orwell's 1945 allegorical "beast fable": "the pigs are walking, the pigs are walking!" — an indication of corrupt leadership. Arzt perceives that Jack, John and Kate, the apparent leaders of the group, are acting suspiciously and dishonestly ("Expose").

*A Brief History of Time: From the Big Bang to Black Holes,** Stephen Hawking

This nonfiction work by renowned physicist Stephen Hawking posits questions of the origin of the universe in lay terms, exploring the author's own attempts to develop a "grand unifying theory" (GUT). Though not a subject of literary fiction, this popular work deals with many scientific concepts that have been addressed in the series such as time travel, black holes and the death of the universe. Its appearance may serve as a clue to isolating *Lost*'s generic identity as science fiction, but the book also contains several profound passages that add significance to a cultural analysis of *Lost*. One such line from *A Briefer History of Time*, an even more condensed version of the original work, follows: "The discovery of a complete and unified theory, therefore, may not aid the survival of our species . . . But ever since the dawn of civilization, people have not been content to see events as unconnected and inexplicable. We have craved an understanding of the underlying order in the world." This notion, applied to the *Lost* fandom, explains much about the viewers' desire to connect the pieces, find greater meaning and employ a single theory to unlock the mystery of a fictional universe, "and our goal is nothing less than a complete description of the universe we live in" (18).

Aldo, an "Other," is seen reading *A Brief History of Time* in "Not in Portland," as he guards Room 23 where Karl is prisoner. He seems to be reading a section about black holes and the event horizon. The book is also shown in "The Man From Tallahassee" in Ben's house.

Carrie, Stephen King

Carrie is a horror novel about an awkward teenage girl, mercilessly teased by her peers and oppressed by her fanatically religious mother. She uses her telekinetic powers to carry out acts of vengeance initially directed at only her schoolmates, but ultimately her wrath is unleashed on the entire town.

This book is the topic of a heated discussion at the Others' book club, shortly before the plane crash in the first episode of season three. Adam claims that the work is genre fiction, not "real literature." He calls it "by-the-numbers religious hokum-pokum" and implies that Ben dislikes this kind of "science fiction" ("A Tale of Two Cities"). Juliet says that it's her favorite book, which might reflect the writers' sentiments about Stephen King's work in general.

The Coalwood Way, Homer Hickam

This memoir chronicles one summer in Hickam's hometown of Coalwood, West Virginia, when he was 16 years old.

The Coalwood Way can be seen in a Dharma classroom when the hostiles attack in "The Man Behind the Curtain."

Dark Horse, Tami Hoag

In this suspense thriller, Elena Estes, a tough ex-cop, gets involved in a sinister side of the competitive equestrian sports world.

The book can be seen on Jack's bookshelf in "Tale of Two Cities."

Dirty Work, Stuart Woods

Stone Barrington is an attorney working on an undercover case among Manhattan's elite class. The assignment begins as an investigation into alleged infidelity, but the accused spouse turns up murdered one night, leaving Barrington in a suspicious position.

Dirty Work appears in "A Tale of Two Cities" next to Sawyer's recovery bunk in the Swan station.

Evil Under the Sun, Agatha Christie

Sawyer is reading this murder mystery in "Expose" when Nikki approaches. The episode title is suggestive of a melodramatic suspense novel and the episode itself is an odd murder mystery of sorts, considering Nikki and Paolo are buried alive.

The Fountainhead, Ayn Rand

Howard Roark, the novel's protagonist, is a model of Rand's vision of the ideal rugged individual. He possesses the three characteristics that define her philosophy of objectivism: reason, purpose and self-esteem. The story follows Roark's career as an architect in New York City, underscoring the strength of ego as he struggles to keep his personal values intact among the pressure of outside influences. This resistance to change is a distinctive feature of Rand's work, in which the central character is unchanged despite extensive narrative conflict.

Damon Lindelof compared Sawyer to Roark in a special feature of the season three DVD set, "The Lost Book Club." Indeed, it is Sawyer who is seen reading this novel on the beach in "Par Avion."

Harry Potter, J. K. Rowling

Viewers can see *Harry Potter and the Prisoner of Azkaban*, the third book of J. K. Rowling's popular series, on Jack's shelf in "A Tale of Two Cities." The story's similarities include a sprawling mythology and what Jason Mittel calls a "unity of purpose" (Mittel 2009, 125). One important theme that *Harry Potter* shares with *Lost* is the idea of being "chosen" for a greater cause, as seen in the messianic promises that surround characters like Locke and Aaron.

Hotel, Arthur Hailey

A copy of *Hotel* is found on Ben's bookshelf in "Through the Looking Glass." The St. Gregory Hotel in New Orleans is the setting and centerpiece of this novel in the same way that the island is central to the narrative of *Lost*. Each of *Hotel*'s characters has a troubled past and is working through his conflicts and towards redemption.

Jurassic Park, Michael Crichton

A tale about biological experimentation gone awry, this Crichton thriller follows a team of scientific pioneers who have successfully recreated dinosaurs. They develop a dinosaur theme park on an island preserve, but by the time they realize that the dinosaurs are out of control, it is too late to reverse the effects of their cloning project.

Nikki references this novel in "Expose": "This isn't Jurassic Park, Paolo."

Laughter in the Dark, Vladimir Nabokov

This novel tells the story of Albinus, a man tragically obsessed with a woman several years his junior. The narrator provides the entire plot of the story in a brief paragraph on the first page. He then fleshes out the self-destructive relationship to which Albinus has succumbed. This work demonstrates nonlinear storytelling, something with which viewers are familiar in *Lost*.

Hurley is seen reading Nabokov's work in "Flashes Before Your Eyes."

Left Behind, Tim LaHaye and Jerry Jenkins

This series of stories by fundamentalist Christian writers LaHaye and Jenkins chronicles the apocalypse as prophesied in the New Testament's book of Revelations. Notably, the characters' actions don't have any effect on the predicted course of events and many times they unwittingly facilitate the fulfillment of a prophecy.

Along the same lines, *Lost* characters question whether their individual actions can change fate. Are they exercising their free will or are their actions already predetermined?

"Left Behind" is the title of episode fifteen in season three.

The Oath, John Lescroart

Part of a series, this legal mystery thriller about murder, corruption and healthcare is seen in Ben's tent in "The Brig" when Locke discusses with Ben the murder of his father.

On Writing, Stephen King

This nonfiction work serves as an inspirational memoir for aspiring writers.

King describes a white rabbit with the number "8" printed on it to explain the power of descriptive detail in writing. In "Every Man for Himself" Ben conducts an experiment on Sawyer using a number 8 white rabbit.

Rick Romer's Vision of Astrology, Rick Romer

This is a fictitious book that Claire is seen reading in "Left Behind."

The Stone Leopard, Colin Forbes

This spy novel, set in France in 1975, dramatizes a political conspiracy when a World War II resistance leader is found alive.
The Stone Leopard is seen on the bookshelf when the Dharma Initiative is attacked by the Hostiles in "The Man Behind the Curtain."

Stranger in a Strange Land, Robert Heinlein

First published in 1961, this science-fiction novel was received with some controversy because of the protagonist's defense of such contentious ideas as public fornication and agnosticism. The central character, Valentine Michael Smith, is raised by Martians and then returned to Earth as an adult. The story chronicles his attempts to assimilate into human culture and his struggle to understand the social and emotional standards of humanity.

The title of the book originates in the book of Exodus: "She [Zippo'rah] bore him a son, whom he named Gershom: for he said, I am a stranger in a foreign land" (2.22, NAB). In many translations the phrase "stranger in a strange land" is used.

"Stranger in a Strange Land" is the title of season three's ninth episode.

Robert Heinlein's stories are a strong component of *Lost*'s science-fiction heritage. (See "By His Bootstraps"* in Chapter 5.)

A Tale of Two Cities,* Charles Dickens

One of Charles Dickens' most famous works, this novel's title is used as the season three premiere episode title to illustrate the differences between the two groups on the island — the survivors and the Others. The relationship between France and England in Dickens' novel is a tenuous reflection of island life as viewers know it in *Lost*, but the writers have pointed to Charles Dickens' style of episodic literature as a precursor to serialized television drama. (See more on this novel in Chapter 7.)

Through the Looking-Glass and What Alice Found There,* Lewis Carroll

In Lewis Carroll's sequel to *Alice's Adventures in Wonderland*, *Through the Looking-Glass and What Alice Found There*, the young protagonist reads "Jabberwocky," a nonsensical poem about a boy who slays and beheads a dragon-like creature. *Lost*'s smoke monster is reminiscent of this fictional beast, the Jabberwock, with its "eyes of flame . . . whiffling through the tulgey wood." This comparison is one of the less obvious examples of how Carroll's stories are deeply woven into the fabric of *Lost*. The story of Alice is a fundamental starting point for examining how the show incorporates traditional literature into its narrative and how those works expand the story beyond the medium of television.

When Alice first enters the world beyond the looking glass and looks "out in all directions over the country" (39) she notices that it is all laid out like a giant chess board as far as she can see. "It's a great huge game of chess that's being played all over the world — if this is the world at all, you know."

This is the title of the last episode of season three when the Looking Glass station, an underwater Dharma station, becomes a central part of the narrative.

To Kill a Mockingbird, Harper Lee

Juliet tells Jack she is going to show the 1962 film adaptation of this novel in "The Cost of Living."

Valhalla Rising, Clive Cussler

Published in 2001, this suspense novel is the protagonist's sixteenth book in Cussler's adventure series. Set in the present day amid a search and rescue mission, the story contains references to mythology and famous literary characters like Jules Verne's Captain Nemo.

The novel can be seen on Ben's bookshelf in "Through the Looking Glass."

Season four books

Captain Gault, Being the Exceedingly Private Log of a Sea-Captain, William Hope Hodgson

This is a collection of stories about the adventures of a fictional sea captain. It was published in 1917.

Captain Gault is the name of the Australian captain of the freighter, *Kahana*, featured in the episode titled "Ji Yeon."

Catch-22, Joseph Heller

Viewers might remember the book that Hurley, Charlie and Desmond recovered from Naomi's pack when she first landed on the island: *Ardil-22* (episode "Catch-22"). This is a French translation of Joseph Heller's wartime novel that spawned the term "catch-22." The expression is commonly used to convey a set of circumstances in which any one of the available options will result in a negative outcome. This type of situation is illustrated many times in the series, especially when it comes to a character's moral dilemmas. For instance, should Sun save Michael by translating the misunderstanding between him and Jin ("House of the Rising Sun"), revealing an important secret that might destroy her marriage? Or should she save herself and leave Michael to fend for himself? And then there is Michael's own catch-22: should he put his fellow castaways in danger to save his son? Or should he prolong his son's captivity and keep his friends safe?

Captain John Yossarian, a bombardier based on the fictitious island of Pianosa during World War II, faces a legal loophole that dictates he must follow the orders of his commanding officer, even if they contradict the Air Force's rules. When his superior tells him he must fly double the required 40 missions, he is legally, though unfairly, obligated to complete them. When he tries to be excused from his military duties by feigning insanity he is again informed of Catch-22 which states that "anyone who wants to get out of combat duty isn't really crazy" (Heller).

The Holy Qur'an

A sacred text of the Muslim faith, Qur'an means "recitation." Followers of Islam consider it to be a divinely inspired book. It is the word of God written by Muhammad through the "recitation" of the angel Gabriel. "Indeed, it is a noble Qur'an, in a treasured book, touched only by the purified" (56.77–79).

A copy of the Qur'an is seen in "The Economist" on the shelf in front of Ben's hidden room.

The Invention of Morel, Adolfo Bioy Casares

This novella revolves around a contraption that captures reality and repeatedly "plays it back." The inventor, Morel, has engineered an experiment in which his subjects can live certain moments again and again, for eternity. The novel, by Argentinean writer Adolfo Bioy Casares, is told through the diary of a fugitive living on an island. He observes a group of people who mysteriously appear on the island but then disappear and reappear every so often. They are the subjects of Morel's experiment that took place several years prior to the time in which the fugitive arrives on the island.

Sawyer is seen reading this novella in the episode "Eggtown." The island's uncanny properties that seem to produce ghosts, and that have created insanity among some visitors, are reminiscent of *Lost*'s island.

Kings of Love: The Poetry and History of the Ni'matullahi Sufi Order, Nasrollah Pūrjavādī and Peter Lamborn Wilson (translators)

This history of Ni'matullah's teachings and collection of Sufi poetry was seen on Ben's bookshelf in "The Economist."

Manservant and Maidservant, Ivy Compton-Burnett

Published in 1947, this is the story of Horace Lamb, a cruel man who under-goes a transformation and wants to repent for his past transgressions.

After a chilling nightmare scene in which a ghostly Claire visits Aaron, Kate grabs a gun that is lying on top of this book ("There's No Place Like Home").

On the Road, Jack Kerouac

This classic American story depicts America's "beat" generation through the eyes of Sal Paradise. It illustrates the rejection of tradition and institutions and depicts travel as a means to liberation. Dean Moriarty embodies this revolutionary sense of freedom more than any of the characters.

Ben uses the name Dean Moriarty as a pseudonym when he checks into the Tunisian hotel in "The Shape of Things to Come."

The Shape of Things to Come,* H. G. Wells

After his death, Dr. Philip Raven leaves behind a "dream book" that tells the future, from his death until the year 2105. It is "a history of the future" and foretells many of the twentieth century's real-life global tragedies, including World War II. Considering this book was published in 1933, Wells created not only a good science-fiction novel, but also a prophetic work.

This is the title of episode nine of season four.

The Sheltering Sky, Paul Bowles

This novel, set mostly in the Sahara Desert, can be seen on Ben's shelf in "Eggtown." In it, a couple seeking out the exotic landscape of Morocco for adventure and change, quickly become aware of the dangers that lie in store for foreign travelers.

Tennessee Williams, in a *New York Times* review, describes the novel thus: "In this external aspect the novel is, therefore, an account of startling adventure. In its interior aspect, 'The Sheltering Sky' is an allegory of the spiritual adventure of the fully conscious person into modern experience."

The Shining, Stephen King

A family moves into a haunted Colorado resort when Jack, the father, takes a seasonal job as a hotelkeeper. The dwelling reveals that Jack's young son has clairvoyant powers, but Jack is weakened by his addiction to alcohol and succumbs to the hotel's malevolent paranormal forces.

In "Meet Kevin Johnson" Michael is compared to the novel's protagonist when Minkowski finds him incessantly bouncing a ball against the wall. "What, are you going Nicholson on us?" he asks Michael. In the film version, Jack Torrance, played by Jack Nicholson, bounces the balls against the wall before attempting to murder his family.

Slaughterhouse-Five,* Kurt Vonnegut

At the age of 46, protagonist Billy Pilgrim realizes that he has been chosen to proclaim Tralfamadorian wisdom to all Earthlings. He believes he was meant to provide "corrective lenses" to those who cannot see the true nature of time, which, for Tralfamadorians, is like viewing a mountain range, where all points of time can be seen at once. Billy believes that he will alleviate the suffering of humans by helping them to realize that all things are predestined. Time is a loop — everything that is happening already happened and will happen again — and Billy Pilgrim's single purpose in life is to spread this gospel of Tralfamadorian predetermination.

Although John Locke's purpose is not as clear, he does share with Billy a transformation of character through the sudden epiphany of a cosmic calling. They both understand that everyone was brought to the island (also known as life) for a reason, whether to push a button or to kill an Other.

Desmond makes a direct reference to this novel when he claims that he has become "unstuck in time." The first line of the novel's chapter 1 reads: "Billy Pilgrim has become unstuck in time." Desmond's time-altered experiences and the time traveling of Daniel Faraday's experimental subjects is similar to the way in which Billy Pilgrim's consciousness moves through the time–space continuum.

In "Meet Kevin Johnson" the book and its author are mentioned in a game show that Michael is watching.

See more on this novel in Chapters 2 and 4.

The Survivors of the Chancellor, Jules Verne

Verne is considered to be one of the founding fathers of what is now known as science fiction. In this seafaring adventure, a British ship named the *Chancellor* sails its last voyage. During the long and difficult passage, crew members commit suicide and face the threat of an explosion on board. Only 11 of the original 28 passengers and crew members survive.

On the freighter Regina is seen reading this novel before she commits suicide in "Ji Yeon."

Another Jules Verne novel, *The Mysterious Island*, book three of his famous trilogy, tells the story of five prisoners of war who escape a Confederate prison and steal a hot air balloon. The balloon crashes on Captain Nemo's island where they encounter conflict with the current residents. A possible reference to the book is Shannon's "Mystery frickin' island" comment, which could have been unintentional on the writers' part. Other similarities to the show include a submarine, a cable that leads the colonists to the hidden submarine (similar to the cable that leads to the Looking Glass station) and a dog companion with an uncanny connection to the island.

The Tempest, William Shakespeare

The name of a Dharma station takes its name from this famous work and the play shares a common set of circumstances with *Lost*:

castaways find themselves on a remote island where they must contend with mysterious forces, monsters and spirits. When Benjamin Linus turns against the Dharma Initiative, he uses the Tempest station to release a deadly gas across the island, killing everyone without a gas mask ("The Other Woman").

*VALIS,** Philip K. Dick

This science-fiction novel is based on the author's own religious experience. In the story, it is a pink beam of light that inspires the central character, Horselover Fat, to embark on a convoluted spiritual quest. *VALIS* is a story about faith, the illusion of reality and the nature of time.

John brings this book to Ben in the basement ("Eggtown") where he is being held prisoner. John suggests Ben reread it saying, "You might catch something you missed, the second time around." It is also seen in "The Other Woman" when Ben is reading it.

See more on this novel in Chapters 2 and 6.

Season five books

Caravan of Dreams, Idries Shah

This work is a collection of folklore, philosophical teaching tales and traditional religious stories originating from a Muslim tradition. It can be seen on Ben's bookshelf in "Dead is Dead."

*Everything that Rises Must Converge,** Flannery O'Connor

Jacob is seen reading this collection of short stories outside the apartment where Anthony Cooper pushes John out of the window. He is sitting on a park bench reading when John falls to his doom in "The Incident, Part 2."

Carlton Cuse once remarked that Flannery O'Connor's works have greatly influenced his own writing and *Lost* specifically. "We have a lot of religious themes and sudden and striking violence and she was the master at that. I love her work" (Bradner 2009).

In this collection, one story stands out from the others in the context of this episode: "The Lame Shall Enter First." It is the story of a man named Sheppard who works at a boys' reformatory. He tries desperately to "save" one of the boys from a life of crime, while neglecting the needs of his own son who eventually commits suicide. The name similarity aside, Jack has been known to neglect domestic obligations while trying to save a patient or fix a situation.

Another story from this collection, "Revelation" is also significant to *Lost*, as demonstrated in Chapter 2.

Fahrenheit 451, Ray Bradbury

This dystopian novel, found on Ben's shelf in "Dead is Dead," shares themes with other *Lost* books listed here, including *Animal Farm* by George Orwell and *Island* by Aldous Huxley. It is the tale of a dismal future when reading is illegal and all books are required to be burned. The main character is a "fireman" whose job it is to set fire to any printed material. His wife spends her days engaged in a mind-numbing 3-D interactive television program. This sets up an interesting juxtaposition in terms of the relationship between television audiences and literature. Can a person be both a consumer of television media and a serious reader? Are audiovisual narratives potential tools for controlling viewers?

Though never directly referenced, Ray Bradbury's short story, "A Sound of Thunder,"* is a significant precursor to *Lost* and many other texts that incorporate time travel into their storylines. See Chapter 4 for more about time travel and for a full description of this short story.

Flowers for Algernon, Daniel Keyes

This novel, seen on Ben's shelf in "Dead is Dead," is the story of an ethically problematic science experiment conducted for the purpose of increasing intelligence. The first subject is a lab mouse named Algernon. Scientists proceed to experiment with humans, starting with Charlie, a man with a very low IQ. The initial result is successful but eventually the effect wears off, leaving Charlie with a great sense of loss.

Daniel Faraday's experimentation with time travel and manipulation of the human brain echoes the moral dilemmas that arise in *Flowers for Algernon*. He conducts trials on a mouse (notably named Eloise) but when he proceeds to test a human subject, the effects are devastating.

The Little Prince, Antoine de Saint-Exupery

This densely illustrated children's novel begins with a man whose airplane crashes in the Sudan. There, he meets a boy from a different planet who has been traveling through the universe. The boy has many tales to tell the aviator, mostly about absurd characters, each living on his own planet. This "Little Prince" has left his home, an asteroid named B612, after being spurned by the planet's only flower and the boy's singular source of companionship.

"Besixdouz" (B612) is also the name of Rousseau and crew's science expedition boat, shown during one of the time hiccups, supposedly when the island "landed" in 1988.

"The Little Prince" is the title of the fourth episode of season five, one that follows the fate of Aaron after the Oceanic Six are rescued. Viewers can assume that the "prince" is Aaron, a blond child engaged in jet-setting adventures at a young age and coming into contact with a various array of dysfunctional adult figures.

Mysteries of the Ancient Americas: The New World before Columbus, Reader's Digest Staff

A nonfiction text that young Juliet is seen reading in a flashback in "The Incident," this is an historical account of the first settlers to the "New World" and the lost cities of the Americas, written for young readers.

Roots, Alex Haley

Roots is a work of fiction about one family's legacy of enslavement and African heritage, written by a man who has claimed to trace his own "roots" back to a particular village in Gambia.

This book is seen on Ben's bookshelf in "Dead is Dead."

A Separate Reality, Carlos Castaneda

This work of "nonfiction" chronicles Castaneda's experiences with don Juan Matus, a shaman or "Yaqui Indian sorcerer," and records the philosophical conclusions to which Castaneda arrives because of these experiences.

Young Ben offers this book to an imprisoned Sayid in "He's Our You." This episode features the apparent use of psychoactive drugs, a prominent part of don Juan Matus's practices according to Castaneda.

Ulysses, James Joyce

This extremely detailed chronicle of one day in the life of Leopold Bloom and Stephen Dedalus is composed of puzzles, classical references and quite a few enigmatic passages. The setting is Dublin, June 16, 1904, and the reader, through stream-of-consciousness storytelling, is privy to all of the central character's observations, meals, discussions and musings throughout the 265,000-word day.

Ben is reading this novel on the plane that is scheduled to fly to Guam but is headed for the island in "316." Jack leans over and asks him, "How can you read?"

Ulysses is the Greek form of the name Odysseus. See *The Odyssey* in the section titled "Implied Allusions" later in this chapter.

Uncle Tom's Cabin, Harriet Beecher Stowe

This nineteenth-century anti-slavery novel tells the story of a long-suffering slave and his community. The work had a profound effect on the abolitionist movement in nineteenth-century America.

The book can be seen on Ben's bookshelf in "Dead is Dead."

Season six books

The Chosen, Chaim Potok

In this 1967 novel, two teenage boys in 1940s Brooklyn develop an unlikely friendship. Though they live in the same area and share a common Jewish-American heritage, they meet for the first time in high school, as a result of an accident during a neighborhood baseball game. The novel explores the value of friendship, underscoring the notion that individuals thrive by emotionally investing themselves in community life. Being "chosen" in the context of this novel refers both to the position of the Jews as God's chosen people and the status of Danny Saunders as the eldest male, obligated to inherit his father's position as leader of their Hasidic sect. It also illustrates the contrast between being chosen and choosing, being acted upon and being the actor, recalling the pervading theme of free will versus predetermination in *Lost*.

Ben finds *The Chosen* in Sawyer's old tent on the beach ("Dr. Linus").

Deep River, Shūsaku Endō

Written by a Christian Japanese novelist and published in English in 1994, this novel tells the story of four tourists traveling in India. In the face of conflict they each ultimately discover an individual spiritual purpose for the trip.

Temple-dweller Dogen can be seen reading this book at his desk in "Sundown."

Fear and Trembling,* Søren Kierkegaard

The title comes from the New Testament: "So then, my beloved, obedient as you have always been, not only when I am present but all the more now when I am absent, work out your salvation with fear and trembling" (Phil. 2.12). A copy of this book is found in a backpack when Hurley leads the group under the walls of the temple in "LA X." A work of philosophy, it retells the story of God testing Abraham's faith (Genesis) and explores the ethical implications of a blind duty to God.

See more on this text in Chapter 2.

Haroun and the Sea of Stories, Salman Rushdie

In this children's story, the death of imagination and the silence of a gifted storyteller are the central concerns; the repression of creativity is illustrated in the form of dark forces attempting to poison the "Sea of Stories." Haroun's father, a storyteller, has lost his flair for yarn-spinning and the father-and-son duo travel to Earth's second moon to reclaim his powers. Two societies live on this moon; one lives in complete light and the other in complete darkness. The dark side wants to poison the Sea of Stories and dampen the imaginative forces behind the power of storytellers. But Haroun helps protect the magical waters: ". . . even though he was full of a sense of hopelessness and failure, the magic of the Ocean began to have an effect on Haroun." Rushdie uses allusions familiar to the *Lost* viewer in this work such as references to Lewis Carroll's Alice stories and Frank Baum's *Wonderful Wizard of Oz*.

In "LA X" Desmond is reading this book on the plane.

*Notes From Underground,** Fyodor Dostoevsky

In "Everybody Loves Hugo" as Hurley sifts through Ilana's personal things, he sees a very sandy book: Fyodor Dostoevsky's short novel, in the original Russian. *Notes From Underground* is the story of an unnamed, self-isolated character who tortures himself by trying to identify and strive toward humanity's highest virtues, but eventually realizes that, for all of his well-intentioned philosophizing, his ideas ring hollow and life seems empty. This early existentialist (or, arguably, pre-existentialist) work proposes that the essence of humanity is not goodness or virtue or even personal interest; rather, it is free will that makes us human. The man from underground declares, "One's own free and unfettered volition, one's own caprice, however wild, one's own fancy, inflamed sometimes to the point of madness — that is the one best and greatest good . . . What a man needs is simply and solely independent volition, whatever that independence may cost and wherever it may lead" (Dostoevsky 1972, 11).

The inclusion of this novel hints at an existentialist reading of the series. The characters must exercise their "independent volition" and trust themselves, not an external force or a transcendent being. Ultimately, none of them are holding out for an external savior, nor do they have a clear idea of a fated plan. Each has "no other aim than the one he sets himself," in the words of Jean-Paul Sartre. See more on Sartre and existentialism in Chapter 3.

Tibetan Book of the Dead*

This sacred text is implicitly referenced in both "The Substitute" and "Sundown" in the image of the scale as a tool for judgment in the afterlife. According to Tibetan Buddhism, shortly after death, the soul is faced with a scale — on one side there are black pebbles, on the other white ones. If the scale tips too much in the "wrong direction," the soul will be tortured and punished by the terrifying "Lord of Death." But first, the newly dead must look into a mirror that reflects the "naked soul," including all of its hidden faults and deepest desires. Viewers will recall the magic mirror in the lighthouse where Jack's deep-seated longing to find a true home is revealed to him.

In "Sundown" Dogen tells Sayid that "For every man there is a scale. On one side is good and on the other, evil." Sayid's scale, according to Dogen, is tipped in the wrong direction.

Implied allusions and narrative predecessors

"By His Bootstraps,"* Robert A. Heinlein

This science-fiction novella explores the paradox of time travel. It serves as a good model of corporeal travel as opposed to *Slaughterhouse-Five*, the construct and precursor for Desmond's traveling consciousness. Chapter 4 provides a comparison between Heinlein's implementation of time travel as a narrative device and the time-travel sequence in *Lost*.

The Great Divorce,* C. S. Lewis

This novella constructs a fictionalized vision of the afterlife through one man's dream, carefully focusing on the conversations that he has with "spirits" and "ghosts" in purgatory and heaven.

In light of the series finale, this story is a significant text for a broader understanding of popular images of the afterlife. Although it contains a strictly Christian idea of the universe, it is teeming with interesting perspectives of concepts such as free will, forgiveness and "letting go."

Island,* Aldous Huxley

Huxley's final novel (1963) depicts the fictional island of Pala and its utopian community. The society's founding principles are based on a mixture of Eastern and Western philosophical values and scientific findings. Much of the text is spent in the description of the group's philosophy and its conflict with specific characteristics of Western life. The story begins when Will Farnaby crashes his sailboat on the island of Pala and is found by two of the community's children. The Palanese are very protective of their culture and their natural resources and newspaperman Will Farnaby, along with the rest of the world, poses a threat to their existence. There is a conspiracy under way to take over the island and Farnaby is a willing pawn in the game, until he experiences the healing powers of the island and its people.

The novel begins with a strikingly similar scene to *Lost*'s opening image: Farnaby awakes "with a start" after his crash landing and sees "a glade among trees and the long shadows and slanting lights of an early-morning forest."

Pala is the name of the ferry system on *Lost*'s island, presumably christened by the Dharma Initiative.

The Island of Dr. Moreau, H. G. Wells

A strange persuasion came upon me that . . . I had here before me the whole balance of human nature in miniature form, the whole interplay of instinct, reason and fate in its simplest form.
— H. G. Wells, *The Island of Dr. Moreau*, 149

After a shipwreck and subsequent days at sea, the main character, Prendick, is picked up by a strange crew and brought to an island where malformed half-human, half-animal creatures dwell. Dr. Moreau, a scientist known for his brutal vivisections, reigns supreme over this strange island as creator of the beast people. He fashions new kinds of hybrid animals with the capacity for speech. They stand erect and abide by human-like social constructs such as marriage and "The Law."

Dr. Moreau's efforts can be compared to the scientifically ambitious individuals and teams who are attracted to the island and its unique natural properties. The Dharma Initiative is such an organization and one of its members, Stuart Radzinsky, is notable for his ruthless determination to advance scientific knowledge at all costs. In "The Incident" he insists on continuing to drill at the site of an electromagnetic pocket, without regard for the human lives at stake. He is intent on harnessing the powerful electromagnetism to be used as an energy source. Chang criticizes Radzinsky, warning of the cataclysmic consequences that could result from continued drilling but Radzinsky does not cease, replying that "if Edison had been afraid of the consequences we'd still be sitting in the dark."

The creatures that Dr. Moreau "humanizes" are destined for a crueler fate than brute animal life; they are bound to an existence in which they must "stumble in the shackles of humanity." Moreau is the god of these creatures, but even he is subject to the limitations of animal life. As the castaway narrator eventually concludes, "A blind fate, a vast pitiless mechanism, seemed to cut and shape the fabric of existence" (150).

In a way, this is also *Lost*'s conclusion. Though the central characters are redeemed in a spiritual sense, most of them suffer greatly as a result of their own physical fragility and the calculated forces of other human beings. They face brutal deaths as they are hunted down not only by the

Smoke Monster, but by one another. Naomi, Sayid, Daniel, Jack, Charles Widmore, Dogen, Charlie — these characters "stumbling in the shackles of humanity" find their doom in the "pitiless mechanism" of a cruel wilderness and the brutality of human nature.

Sawyer refers to Daniel Faraday as H. G. Wells in "The Variable" after the scientist (Faraday) attempts to explain some of the finer points of time travel.

(For more on the literature of H. G. Wells, see *The Time Machine* in Chapter 4.)

Lost Horizon,* James Hilton

Because this novel has more in common with *Lost* than almost any other narrative presented in this book, I have provided a more extensive summary.

Like Joseph Conrad's *Heart of Darkness*, this is a story within a story, with a primary narrator set in Berlin's Templehof airport telling the story to two fellow Englishmen. Rutherford, recounts a tale about four passengers of a rescue flight out of Baskul and their journey into the unknown mountainous tundra of Western China.

The central protagonist, Conway, is an English ambassador working in a region of China during a period of civil unrest. He and three other travelers board a plane with the intention of evacuating to Peshawar. They discover that the plane has been hijacked as it heads toward the Tibetan mountains. Eventually the plane crashes, killing the pilot and leaving the others to find their way to civilization. They encounter a search party that leads them to a beautiful, lush valley — Shangri-La — shielded from the brutal conditions of the subfreezing region. They discover that they are prevented from leaving this oasis for several months due to the difficult landscape. They are provided luxurious accommodations and are made to feel welcome.

Conway eventually discovers that he was brought there for a reason — to replace the community's dying leader, the High Lama who is approaching his 200th birthday. When Conway asks why he was brought to Shangri-La, the High Lama responds, "There *is* a reason, and a very definite one indeed" (157).

The relationships in *Lost Horizon* bear a strong resemblance to the ones in *Lost*. John can be compared to Conway and Jack to Mallinson. Conway wants to stay in Shangri-La and fulfill his destiny while Mallinson, a younger, more impetuous man focuses all of his energy on developing a plan of escape. Another survivor, Barnard, is running from the law and is content to remain in the luxury of Shangri-la. This character brings to mind both Sawyer and Kate. The fourth survivor, Miss Brinklow, is a Catholic missionary and eventually decides to stay because of her interest in the region's puzzling spiritual qualities.

The High Lama prophesies a coming war where the strong will devour "each other, the Christian ethic may be fulfilled, and the meek shall inherit the earth" (159).

Eventually, Mallinson leaves the colony and convinces Conway to come with him, a turning point that ends in disaster. The novel ends with a question — does Conway ever make it back to Shangri-La?

Lost: Endangered Species; Lost: Secret Identity; Lost: Signs of Life, Cathy Hapka

These books are novelizations of the series based on the lives of named and unnamed characters in the television version. Three books have been published, presented in a serialized fashion.

The Moon Pool, Abraham Merritt

In the introduction to a recent publication of *The Moon Pool*, Lynnette Porter begins by providing a description of the novel's setting: "A tropical paradise with a hidden portal to another world . . . warring peoples . . . a complex mythology of these peoples' origins and beliefs . . . a philosophical debate" about whether scientific principles or the supernatural can explain the region's strange phenomena (Merritt and Porter 2008).

She is quick to acknowledge that for the modern reader and viewer, this passage is reminiscent of *Lost*. Porter's point, of course, is that *The Moon Pool* is a significant forebear of the series, as well as that of many twentieth and twenty-first century science-fiction stories.

The novel's resemblance to *Lost* is evident: A diverse group of travelers discover an underground lost world full of strange people and occurrences. They access the secret dwelling on a South Pacific island and what they find is both wonderful and horrifying. There is a creature called the Dweller or the Shining One who exerts a great power over its subjects; those who fall under the spell of The Dweller experience extreme pain and astonishing pleasure, alike.

The Odyssey,* Homer

Homer's *Odyssey* is an epic story of one man's homeward-bound journey after a great war fought far from his own island of Ithaca. The hero, Odysseus, faces a long and brutal voyage beset with monsters and other supernatural forces, including the divine nymph, Calypso, who holds him captive on her island. When he finally arrives home, the sole survivor of a difficult passage, 20 years have passed since his departure. Indeed, this classic story is a hero's journey or "monomyth," as romantically defined by Joseph Campbell.[2] Arguably, *Lost* also fits the monomyth construct, along with other mass media "parables" (*Star Wars*, *Lord of the Rings* and *The Matrix*, to name a few).

What follows is a brief set of points that outline notable similarities between *Lost* and *The Odyssey*.

Odysseus and his crew find themselves stranded, more than once, on enchanted islands in uncharted waters. They travel to the underworld, an island surrounded by foreboding waters, notably called the Oceanus River, where Odysseus speaks to several ghosts, including his own mother's. (Jack and Christian's reunion on the island in "White Rabbit" reflects this element of the Odyssey.) The ghost of Odysseus's mother asks him how he, in life, is able to visit the land of the dead. She explains: "it is a hard thing for the living to see these places, for between us and them there are great and terrible waters, and there is Oceanus, which no man can cross on foot . . ." (135). At another point in the story, Odysseus is drawn to another island and held captive by the beautiful and immortal Calypso. Recall John Locke's well-known line from season one: "I've looked into the eye of this island and what I saw was beautiful." Perhaps a Calypso, of sorts, has a hand in this smoke monster sorcery. The island's promise to Locke is akin to Calypso's offering: a new life in the pure, virginal wilderness, a cure for all physical ailments and the possibility of immortality. Another comparable character to Odysseus is Desmond, and not simply because his love interest shares the same name as Penelope, wife of *The Odyssey*'s hero.

Waiting for Godot, Samuel Beckett

This play centers around Vladimir and Estragon, two men who claim to be waiting for someone named Godot. There is little forward action and few explicit messages, but the drama's aimlessness and confusing dialogue are intentional. In this fragmented drama, events and dialogue are continually repeated and revisited. There is no stable concept of time for the characters, yet the various divergent perceptions of time are all considered to be correct. Like everything else in Vladimir and Estragon's world, time is arbitrary and disjointed. Similarly, the narrative of *Lost* becomes confusing and, at times, meaningless, as the viewers' understanding of the nature of time dissolves into confusion.

This work has not been directly referenced in the television program, but the waiting of Jacob and his archrival on the beach in season five clearly reflects the sense of stasis and circularity depicted by the two main characters in Beckett's play. Jacob and his companion discuss a group of voyagers on an incoming ship. They acknowledge the dismal prediction of the visitors, illustrating the fate of humanity: people will inevitably bring about chaos and destruction. But Jacob alone has faith in them and feels that, despite their weaknesses, the visitors are worthy of redemption and, further, that there is a reason for their arrival. His companion is less optimistic. The Man in Black's postmodern perspective aligns with this play's fundamental observation of the human condition — that the search for meaning and purpose in life is a futile undertaking.

2

"Are You There, God?" Faith, Sacrifice and Redemption

God doesn't know how long we've been here, John. He can't see this island any better than the rest of the world can.

— Ben ("Dave")

Now the question has been boiled down to its essential root — is there a God or is there nothingness?

— Damon Lindelof ("The Island Paradox" 2010)

Lost would look very different without its deeply imbedded religious themes and ongoing discussion of faith. Though frequently cloaked in secular terms, spiritual concerns figure significantly in the basic fabric of the series; these include the conflict between good and evil, the notion of an afterlife, reincarnation, judgment, redemption, rebirth and the act of sacrifice. That the writers of *Lost* rely on sacred narratives for inspiration is quite obvious. Evidence can be found simply by reviewing some of the episode titles: "Exodus," "Psalm 23," "Fire + Water," "316," "Numbers" and "Left Behind." Consider too, the promotional images for the final season, a collection of cast photos titled "The Lost Supper," in which many of the main characters are seated around a piece of plane wreckage configured to resemble the length of a table. Some are drinking from wine glasses, and Dharma-brand food and drink can be seen on the table. John Locke is seated at the center of the table as a Christ figure.

Rarely in *Lost* do the characters directly address one particular set of religious tenets or explicitly identify a certain deity. A monotheistic notion of "God" is sometimes mentioned but more often the island serves as the most compelling object of faith. In an interview aired during the final season, co-producers Damon Lindelof and Carlton

Cuse were quite clear on this point: "We substituted the phrase 'the island' for the word 'god'" (Cuse and Lindelof 2010). It is the island for which many characters do what they do. Everything that happens in *Lost* revolves around the strength and the mystery of the island, whether the characters are "believers" or not. Even Jack is drawn back to the island for mysterious reasons beyond his comprehension. The sacred works and other stories presented in this chapter provide varying models of divinity to contribute to our understanding of the god or gods of *Lost*. For Philip K. Dick, God is revealed in a pink beam of light; for Flannery O'Connor, God's work can be violent and grotesque; and for C. S. Lewis the line between goodness and evil, heaven and hell, god and godless, is clear and absolute. In this chapter I will explore how a higher power is revealed in *Lost* through various works of fiction and mythology.

Faith

Because it's hell to believe there ain't a hell of a chance.
— Josh Ritter, "Thin Blue Flame," *The Animal Years*

It's never been easy!
— John Locke, "Orientation"

Lost addresses a number of compelling questions about the conflict between faith and reason, as most significantly illustrated by the characters John Locke and Jack Shephard: Can faith be cultivated? Who or what deserves our faith? What is the cost of believing? A memorable scene in "Orientation" conveys the disparity between these two characters and between the notions of faith and skepticism in general. John wants to continue pushing the button in the Swan hatch based on a compelling belief that it is their duty. But without clear evidence that the monitoring process makes any difference,[1] Jack refuses to participate. "It's not real. Look, you want to push the button, you do it yourself." What follows is a revelation of both viewpoints: John posits the question, "Why do you find it so hard to believe?" and Jack quickly retorts, "Why do you find it so easy?"

Some viewers have speculated that season five's episode "316" refers back to season three, episode sixteen, "One of Us." Others conjecture that it is named for the biblical passage John 3.16, which reads, "For god so loved the world that he gave his only son so that everyone who believes in him might not perish but have eternal life." Knowing the writers' taste for complexity and ambiguity, the title almost certainly refers to both, but here I will address the New Testament's influence. The key words for *Lost* in this quotation are "believes in him" and "may have eternal life." The island seems to offer a chance for immortality or prolonged life to those who believe and stay. For those who doubt, the island puts forward a tough obstacle course of life-changing challenges. For those who lack the ability to embrace mystery (e.g. Jack Shephard), it provides the opportunity for transformation.

The episode "316" is permeated by Christian iconography and significant biblical themes. A contributor to *Lostpedia* has noted that even the opening scene of this episode is a vague reference to the first chapter of C. S. Lewis's *Prince Caspian*, "The Island," where the children play in the water when they first arrive (*Chronicles of Narnia* 2009). The other allusion to the Narnia series is the disclosure of a new Dharma station, the Lamp Post. In the world of Narnia, a lamppost marks the threshold from one world to the next. Consider the conversation between Ben and Jack at the Lamp Post headquarters, which is disguised as a church. They are standing in front of a sacred painting, a rendering of Thomas the Apostle when Ben explains that this particular disciple "refused to acknowledge the resurrection. He just couldn't wrap his mind around it. The story goes . . . that he needed to touch Jesus' wounds to be convinced."

> Jack: So was he?
> Ben: Of course he was. We're all convinced sooner or later,
>   Jack.

If the apostle needs what amounts to scientific evidence to believe, then he is an ideal comparison to Jack. He and Thomas are kindred spirits, both skeptical men by nature, and Ben's reference here foretells Jack's ultimate transformation to a man of faith.

The Book of Job

The story of Job is analogous to John Locke's life in terms of faith, but also presents a model for Richard Alpert's experience on the island, in the grip of Jacob and the Man in Black's high-stakes game. Job's story chronicles the test of the human spirit, illustrated by one exemplary figure, according to God's standards. The story is structured around a debate between God and Satan about the fundamental nature of human beings. Satan challenges God's faith in man, claiming that people are inherently wicked; Job only appears to be a good man because he is wealthy, secure and supported by family and friends. If he were confronted by poverty, loneliness or illness, Satan argues, Job would curse God and turn away. In short, Satan believes that even the most admirable of men can sustain only a very fragile faith.

At certain times, Jacob and the Man in Black are comparable to God and Satan as they are represented in this book: they are like two young boys playing a game, using human beings as game pieces. Job's faith in God is tested as Satan is given free rein to influence Job and lead him astray, not through temptation but through suffering. He destroys Job's wealth, kills his children and makes him an outcast among friends, leaving him with nothing. Richard Alpert is similarly tested even before he arrives on the island — his wife dies and his freedom is taken away when he is sold into slavery. He continues to suffer when the Smoke Monster deceives him into believing that he is in hell and that his wife has been taken by "el Diablo," the devil. Richard is manipulated by the Man in Black and then is granted eternal life by Jacob — the Smoke Monster cannot kill him, which is similar to the one rule that Satan must follow during the test: Job cannot die in the process. But Jacob persuades Richard to follow him and rewards his faith by bestowing upon him a special status. Notably, his subsequent 140 years on the island is equal to the amount of time Job lives after his own trial is over. Consider Robert Sutherland's take on the book of Job: "Such is God's faith in mankind that God chooses to pick up the gauntlet. He elects trial by ordeal to establish the principle that righteousness can exist separately from reward. He chooses Job, humanity's best representative, to be his champion" (Sutherland 2004, 36). Likewise, Jacob chooses not only Richard but several "candidates," those whom he believes will prove the worthiness of the human race.

Kierkegaard, Abraham and Benjamin Linus

Søren Kierkegaard's notion of Christian faith is demonstrated in the philosophical work *Fear and Trembling*, which points its reader back to both New and Old Testaments. Hurley finds a copy of this book in the backpack of a long-dead French castaway, while leading his group under the walls of the temple in "LA X, Part 1." In the book, Kierkegaard retells the story of Abraham's test and explores the nature of faith and the ethical implications of a blind duty to God. He provides four re-renderings of the binding of Isaac, the story in which Abraham is instructed by God to sacrifice the child that he and his wife, Sarah, had long awaited (Gen. 22.1–24). Kierkegaard's work is an exploration of the various outcomes of different actions (Kierkegaard, *Fear and Trembling; Repetition* 1983).

As indicated in Chapter 1, the title of this work comes from the New Testament: "So then, my beloved . . . work out your salvation with fear and trembling." The passage goes on to say, "do everything without grumbling or questioning" (Phil. 2.12). In *Lost*, these words reflect Ben's rhetoric and his unquestioning faith in the island. When Ben's faith in Jacob (and the island) is shaken, he is driven to madness and murders Jacob, the man he worshiped for most of his life. In "The Incident" the Smoke Monster, in the form of John Locke, persuades Ben to question Jacob. When Ben asks, "Why do you want me to kill Jacob?" Locke reminds Ben of his unrequited loyalty to Jacob. He deliberately rattles Ben's faith by pointing out, "you did all this in the name of a man you'd never even met." These sentiments stand in stark contrast to the nature of the original John Locke, a fervent disciple of the island who is known for his great acts of faith and a trust in others that borders on gullibility.

Kierkegaard's work examines the questions that arise from God's request for Abraham to sacrifice his only son. The story addresses the notion of human sacrifice, never realized in Genesis, but still an unspeakable act in the eyes of modern-day readers. In the words of the New American Bible, God tells Abraham it is a "holocaust." *Fear and Trembling* explores the nature of suffering and faith by retelling the story and exposing the emotional impact that this act of faith would bring about.

In the character of Benjamin Linus viewers can clearly see the pain and sacrifice of a deeply embedded faith. Though misguided, his conviction in the island runs deep because, like Isaac, he was saved from death by "holy" powers beyond his understanding. As a child, a dying Ben Linus is revived and brought to life by the Others, presumably through the healing waters of the island. But Ben is also like Abraham: his acts of devotion rival those of the religious patriarch as demonstrated by his lifelong sacrifice to Jacob. He allows Alex, his adopted daughter, whom he loves dearly, to be slaughtered right before his eyes. Unlike Abraham's God, the island does not save her and, ultimately, Ben bears the blame of this particular "holocaust." There is also the act of mass murder that Ben leads in 1992, killing the entire Dharma community, including, in an ironic reversal of child sacrifice, his own father. He initiates the massacre of an entire community, commits patricide and, later, neglects his duty as a father, all in the name of the island. Quite obviously, Ben's sense of duty blinds him in the same way that some religious followers can be led astray through their own sense of conviction. As the series came to an end, it became clear that it was not Jacob or the island that was guiding Ben. The messages Ben receives from his "god" are a confusing amalgamation of directives filtered through Richard Alpert and the Smoke Monster, and exacerbated by Ben's own weaknesses.

Revelation: violent acts of grace

In "The Incident" Jacob sits, calm and composed, reading a collection of short stories by Flannery O'Connor, *Everything That Rises Must Converge*. At the end of season five, much speculation developed among fans over the title of this book, including theories about two separate timelines "converging" and John Locke's potential "convergence" with higher powers. In the background of this scene, a man suddenly crashes through a window and falls several stories to the ground, landing on his back. Viewers know that this man is John Locke and that it was his own father, Anthony Cooper, who just pushed him out of the window. The same turn of events was presented in season one from another perspective.

This shocking course of events in the midst of an otherwise serene day can be likened to the sudden acts of violence in Flannery O'Connor's fiction. O'Connor, a self-described "Catholic writer," conveyed the grace of God by using grotesque images and unexpected acts of aggression in her fiction. As seen in Chapter 1, Carlton Cuse, also a Catholic, noted Flannery O'Connor as his greatest influence. To be sure, in the short stories featured in *Everything That Rises Must Converge* there is no shortage of bizarre and violent acts.

The collection of short stories was O'Connor's last published material before her death in 1967. It has been said that these later works were influenced by Teilhard de Chardin's ideas on the evolution of human consciousness. According to Steven Watkins, "The gist of this Teilhardian idea is that human beings evolve throughout time developing a propensity towards psychic development as they journey towards a destination called Point Omega" (Watkins 2005). De Chardin coined the phrase "everything that rises must converge" based on this theory.

Aside from the title, the stories themselves also share significant themes with *Lost*. Consider "Revelation," the story of Mrs. Turpin, a decidedly self-righteous woman who, to the reader's amusement, continually congratulates herself on her station in life. The audience is privy to her thoughts: she thanks Jesus for not making her "white trash" or a "nigger," and pointedly classifies people according to their skin color and wealth. Sitting in a busy doctor's waiting room, she silently appraises the people around her, ranking them according to their clothes and behavior. All the while, a young woman with a face "blue with acne" glares at her, leaving Mrs. Turpin mystified. The stranger continues to stare in hatred, until Mrs. Turpin says, "When I think who all I could have been besides myself and what all I got, a little of everything, and a good disposition besides, I feel like shouting, 'Thank you Jesus, for making everything the way it is!'" This comment incites the young woman to throw a large book across the room, hitting Mrs. Turpin just above the eye. She then attacks the older woman, attempts to strangle her and says, "Go back to hell where you came from, you old warthog." Initially, Mrs. Turpin is shocked, but eventually she experiences a revelation, in which God shows her a host of souls rising toward heaven — all types of people from all walks of life including "white trash, freaks and lunatics" (O'Connor 1995, 392). There were the more "respectable" people too, the group in which she imagines she is a member. But she "could see by their shocked and altered faces that even their virtues were being burned away" (393).

Like Mrs. Turpin who considers herself to be quite virtuous, Benjamin Linus is a Pharisean character, the kind with which O'Connor was most preoccupied in her fiction. He is like a Pharisee or a false prophet, seemingly a follower of Jacob and leader of "the good guys" as he says, but greatly misled as demonstrated by his sometimes unwitting participation in the darker exploits of the island, and his familiarity with the Smoke Monster. One revelatory moment for him is an extremely violent and shocking scene that takes place when his adopted daughter, Alex, is shot in the head by Martin Keamy, mercenary soldier of Charles Widmore. Like Mrs. Turpin, it takes Ben Linus a disturbing act of brutality to make him reconsider his moral fiber; but as viewers know, Ben requires a continuous stream of revelations to penetrate his corrupt nature.

Unexpected acts of surprising violence have played a prominent role throughout the series, starting with the shock of the plane crash. John Locke is confronted with revelation, first as the survivor of the crash and beneficiary of a miraculous healing and second, in his close encounter with the mysteries of the island. Desmond experiences visions in a series of revelations after the explosion of the hatch. Ben seems transformed after facing the ghost of his daughter through the Smoke Monster's dramatic illusions. Jack comes to terms with his own destiny when he returns to the island and witnesses the violent acts of the Smoke Monster. But the most striking revelations occur in the afterlife scenes of season six. Charlie drives Desmond off of a pier to show him the nature of their true existence; Desmond plows into a wheelchair-bound John Locke; even the birth of Aaron in this purgatorial reality can be considered a violent act of grace — a physical trauma that leads to a powerful bond.

Still, in the characters' "real" lives, the island provides countless opportunities for them to be transformed in the tradition of O'Connor's works. The day-to-day struggle of survival urges each individual to come to terms with his or her weaknesses and past transgressions, and to contemplate the existence of a higher power.

Saviors

VALIS is an acronym for Vast Active Living Intelligence System, a fictional entity loosely based on science-fiction writer Philip K. Dick's life-changing experience in 1974. Of it, Dick says, "It seized me entirely, lifting me from the limitations of the space–time matrix; it mastered me as, at the same time, I knew that the world around me was cardboard, a fake (Sutin 2003). *VALIS*, the first book in a trilogy, follows Horselover Fat, Dick's alter ego, through a mental breakdown and a subsequent spiritual quest in which he and his friends search for the next messiah. Horselover claims that the reality we know is just an illusion and that there is a real universe just beyond the threshold of the known world. The work is complex, thick with cultural allusions to the Gnosis texts, operas and films alike. There is no summing up the plot in a clear and simple manner, but the novel's themes and mythology are revealing of *Lost*'s spiritual message.

The characters of *VALIS* are on a well-worn quest for "the truth" but they use non-traditional devices such as a popular film and a two-year-old child to achieve their means. Initially they want an external savior to provide them full enlightenment. However, it becomes clear to the reader that this adventure may lead them back into themselves. "I don't dare tell Fat that he is searching for himself. He is not ready to entertain such a notion, because, like the rest of us he is searching for an external savior" (Dick 1981, 132). The same character suggests that facing oneself as a judge "is not a bad theological idea. You find yourself facing yourself" (129). *Lost*'s characters invariably discover this phenomenon on the island — they become their own judges as they face the truth of their past lives. As illustrated by the flashbacks, the castaways are compelled to turn inward and scrutinize their lives, starting at the very beginning of the series.

VALIS suggests that gods are just representatives of the forces within each human spirit — the good, the evil, the creative, the destructive, the charitable, the jealous, the merciful, the cruel, etc. As the "fifth savior" proclaims, "you are to follow one rule: you are to love one another as you love me and I love you, for this proceeds from the true god, which is yourselves" (198).

Nietzsche, Oz and the illusion of the savior

Friedrich Nietzsche might have applauded the words of the "fifth savior;" he believed that in the wake of "God's death" humans have a great opportunity to act as their own heroes. Though he feared that many people would become nihilists if a widespread recognition of the death of God set in, he hoped that it would open up creative possibilities for the human imagination. People could strengthen their own emotional powers that remain weak under the belief in a supernatural savior. They would be able to acknowledge the value of this life in the material world. In fact, his last philosophical project addresses the "revaluation of all values" and reassesses what it means to be a moral person. *The Wonderful Wizard of Oz*, a well-referenced book in *Lost*, illustrates the death of a savior (through the dismantling of an illusion) and the relinquishment of power and values that follows.

By exposing the man behind the image of the wizard, Dorothy follows a Nietzsche-like model, revealing the diminishment of a god-like figure and an institution's supremacy. This revelation affects her companions and the people of Oz on a profound level by placing authority in their hands. But the notion of an internal savior versus an external one can prove to be a great burden. Those who had faith in the powers of the great Oz now must rely on their own strength, just as the Lion, the Tin Woodman and the Scarecrow are called to do.

The following lines of dialogue dramatize the moment of truth when the wizard is exposed as a fraud. When Toto the dog literally unveils the man who is manipulating the levers on the great Oz machine, all of the characters are surprised by what they see. Dorothy says, "I thought Oz was a great Head."

"And I thought Oz was a lovely Lady," said the Scarecrow.

"And I thought Oz was a terrible Beast," said the Tin Woodman.

"And I thought Oz was a Ball of Fire," exclaimed the Lion.

"No, you are all wrong," said the little man meekly. "I have been making believe."

They have divergent notions of the entity in control of their world but they are all mistaken. Oz is not the savior at all; each individual has the ability to save himself, just as each has his own notion of what a savior would look like. They recognize not only that they already possess the gifts they were seeking, but that their journey has greatly cultivated these gifts, allowing the characters to clearly "find" them as they arrive at their destination.

Several different scenes in *Lost* recall Dorothy's story, most notably times when one or more characters must embark on a journey to obtain answers from another party. Dorothy's meeting with "the great and powerful Oz" resembles the scene when John and Ben visit "Jacob" in the cabin, which appears in the relevantly titled episode "The Man Behind the Curtain," and a season five episode when John leads Ben and others to the statue where Jacob waits. But the mention of *The Wonderful Wizard of Oz* will remind most viewers of the season two episode "One of Them," when Ben first meets the castaways and tries to convince them that his name is Henry Gale and that he crashed on the island in a hot air balloon. Throughout the series, Ben tries to manipulate the castaways by giving a false impression of his power and relying on their ignorance. Like Dorothy and her friends, the castaways all seem to have competing notions about why they are there and what they should believe. At the outset, few of them trust their own intuition and abilities and, consequently, they surrender authority to figures like Ben who are just "making believe."

Redemption

"Letting go" in *The Great Divorce*

In "LA X" the Smoke Monster (in the form of John Locke) expresses his contempt for the real John Locke. He conveys Locke's life and death as utterly pathetic. The heartbreaking comment he makes about John's confusion in his final moments of life seem to convey that this man-monster has nothing but contempt for the "irreparably broken" man. But then the Smoke Monster defends Locke: "He was the only one of them that didn't want to leave. The only one who realized how pitiful the life he'd left behind actually was." The Smoke Monster's depiction of the island's significance illustrates the Christian ideal of the afterlife and man's reluctance to leave behind worldly attachments. John embraces the mystical, spiritual life and rejects the comforts of the world he left behind. He readily engages in the work of the soul when others refuse to "let go."

In particular, this conversation recalls C. S. Lewis's *The Great Divorce*, a response to William Blake's *Marriage of Heaven and Hell*. The term "divorce" refers to a great chasm that exists between heaven and hell according to some Christian theologians. In the preface, Lewis claims that "if we accept Heaven we shall not be able to retain even the smallest and most intimate souvenirs of Hell" (Lewis 1945, 8). But it is not so much the duality of monotheism that makes this story comparable to *Lost* as it is the theme of "letting go." Let us consider a conversation from *The Great Divorce* between a "spirit" of heaven and a "ghost" of Hell. The spirit is attempting to explain to the ghost where he has been dwelling for so long. "Where do you imagine you've been?" asks Dick, the heavenly spirit. "Ah, I see," replies the ghost, "You mean that the grey town . . . with its field for indefinite progress, is, in a sense, Heaven, if only we have eyes to see it?" But what the ghost is unable to see is that the grey town is Hell, "though if you don't go back you may call it Purgatory" (36). The ghost, however, does not want to stay in heaven; he chooses to return to hell, unable to surrender his old identity and his undeveloped understanding of reality.

Redemption in *The Great Divorce* hinges on the individual's ability to disconnect from certain presumptions he holds about his identity. The ghosts who dwell in Purgatory (or Hell) continue their lives of "indefinite progress," never able to fully move on from life on earth, some even continuing to return to their old homes, haunting the living because they cannot move past their deep attachments. In *Lost*, the notions of "letting go" and "moving on" recur throughout the final season, though some characters resist it, knowing they are not ready or believing they are unworthy. An individual's ability to "let go" is a sign that he or she has been redeemed and that he or she is done with the world. In their lives, most of the central characters demonstrate their redemptive quality within the context of the community of castaways.

Redemption through community and sacrifice

You're not alone. Let me help you.

— Kate to Claire ("The End")

Sometimes works of literary fiction tend to dismiss the group or the society as a corrupting factor in the all-important individual. The novel, for instance, depicts the protagonist in a continual state of solitude set in opposition to the community at large. The written story is limited in the scope of voices it can effectively convey; but television, with its potential for long-term storytelling and a large number of central characters, lends itself to the presentation of multiple viewpoints. The audience of a show like *Lost* sees the group as a collective entity and the community effort of the castaways as essential, whereas even in a complex tale like *The Brothers Karamazov* where many perspectives are provided, the individual always seems isolated and apart from others. Still, there are moments in fiction when a character sacrifices himself for the greater good or for someone else. This is when he or she is most powerful, when making that ultimate connection with others.

It is obvious that community, and the interdependency of one another, plays a considerable role in *Lost*. If viewers have learned nothing else about human relationships from the series it is this: the individual's words and actions profoundly affect the group and the group, in turn, has the potential to transform the individual. This phenomenon is a recurring motif — a character redeems him- or herself by sacrificing his or her needs, or even life, for others. Charlie Pace, the washed-up British rock star, demonstrates this through his dramatic reformation from ineffectual wisecracker to protector and, ultimately, willing hero. When he initially arrives on the island, Charlie is a self-absorbed heroin addict with little experience of helping or caring for others. But he becomes a kind of savior and gives up his life in an effort to save the group of castaways. He willingly submits to the act of self-sacrifice. The survivors believe that they must turn off a signal blocking communication to a potential rescue ship. The switch for this signal is located in an underwater station called The Looking Glass. Charlie carries out the mission, even though he knows he will likely die in the process. He drowns so that the others can live. Admittedly, he is motivated more by his affection for Claire and concern for her infant son, Aaron. But the act is unquestionably selfless and one that benefits an entire community of people. Though Charlie is misled and misinformed (turning off the switch does not result in rescue), he takes action in the service of the group and provides them with an important warning ("not Penny's boat"). He demonstrates his redemptive worth; in essence, he has saved his soul, even if this salvation is rendered only through the survival of the others and their memories of him ("Through the Looking Glass").

This pattern of behavior repeats itself in other hero sequences. Sawyer jumps from a helicopter so that the others can escape ("There's No Place Like Home"); Sayid willingly takes a live bomb to the back of a submarine so that others will be protected from the explosion ("The Candidate"). And, most notably, in battling the Smoke Monster and replacing the "cork of life" back into the island's source, Jack saves the island, his friends and, presumably, the entire world.

Judgment and the afterlife

Many sacred texts characterize the condition of death as a physical location, an earthly landmark with recognizable qualities such as "surrounded by waters," as illustrated in Greek mythology or a dark valley, as in the Bible's Psalm 23: "Ye, though I walk through the valley of the shadow of death / I fear no harm for you are at my side; your rod and staff give me courage." Commonly spoken at Christian funerals, this psalm invokes images of the afterlife that are reflected in *Lost*. The island, long compared to purgatory, if only in a metaphorical sense, seems like an ideal spot for "the valley of the shadow of death," filled with spirits that cannot "move on" and darkened by the danger of the Smoke Monster. In "Ab Aeterno" Richard Alpert expresses the fear that he has been dwelling in the afterlife all along. His sudden loss of faith leads him to believe that the island is hell. But *Lost*'s final word on the afterlife turns out to be an off-island image, a familiar and banal backdrop constructed from the lives of the characters. The so-called alternate universe, a typical science-fiction device, turns out to have a metaphysical explanation, as a vision of the afterlife, a place where people find themselves and come together.

Starting in season five the notion of reincarnation is suggested, with an anagram of the term printed on the side of Ben's van: Canton Ranier. In the cycle of reincarnation, according to the *Tibetan Book of the Dead*, (or *The After-Death Experiences on the Bardo Plane, According to Lāma Kazi Dawa-Samdup's English Rendering*) the soul finds itself in a "between" stage shortly after death. One notable image in this between-life is a scale, containing black pebbles on one side and white pebbles on the other; the black stones represent sinful acts and the white ones reflect good deeds. Viewers will recall that these particular ideas in the cycle of reincarnation are significant to season six. First, there is Dogen's decree: "For every man there is a scale. On one side is good and on the other, evil." The magic mirror in the lighthouse also suggests an association with the Buddhist text; in the mirror Jack's deep-seated longing to find a true home is revealed to him. Another sacred story involving reincarnation and scales is the ancient Egyptian judgment of souls in the underworld, described as "the place where the sun sets each day." There, Anubis weighs the heart of each soul against the weight of a feather and Ammit, a fierce goddess with a head like a crocodile's, eats the souls of those who don't pass the test.

Catch a falling star

> The fifth angel sounded, and I saw a star fall from heaven unto the earth: and to him was given the key of the bottomless pit. And he opened the bottomless pit; and there arose a smoke out of the pit, as the smoke of a great furnace; and the sun and the air were darkened by reason of the smoke of the pit.
> — Rev. 9.1–2

In the season six episode, "Sundown," a spine-chilling rendition of Perry Como's "Catch a Falling Star" serves as the backdrop of the final scene, following the Smoke Monster's slaughter of all temple-dwellers who refuse to follow him. The "falling star" may refer to the Smoke Monster, a Lucifer-esque character who wishes to spread his malevolence to all of the island's inhabitants and to the rest of the world as well.

The name Lucifer, which is Latin for "light-bearing" or "light bringer," was not always synonymous with the term Satan, but according to some Christian sources, Lucifer was a fallen angel, banned from heaven. In Dante Alighieri's *Divine Comedy*, for instance, the plug of earth that was displaced by Lucifer's fall from heaven was thrust up to the surface, forming an island called Purgatory. Volume I, "Inferno," describes Dante's descent into the nine circles of hell where Virgil, the Roman classical poet, serves as tour guide. In this depiction of the afterlife, Lucifer is a prisoner, forever fixed in the ground of the ninth circle of hell (Alighieri 1997). It is suggested that Purgatory is a place that keeps Satan and all evil suppressed, much like *Lost*'s conception of the island as a "cork" that keeps the Smoke Monster restrained.

Dante's adventure is an interesting precursor to *Lost*'s castaway story. Like Dante, the island characters are forced to confront monstrous demons and interact with punished souls as they descend into the various "circles" of the island. Cerberus, for instance, a monster originating in Greek mythology, is also a resident of Dante's Inferno. This creature is described as a "three-headed dog-like beast who guards the gluttons." In *Lost* the vents from which the Smoke Monster escapes are called "cerberus vents" and the Smoke Monster has been referred to as a "security system" or guardian of the island.

Midway on our life's journey, I found myself / In dark woods, the right road lost.

Such begins Dante's allegorical journey, which is fundamentally an exploration of the nature of evil and a medieval rendering of appropriate spiritual punishment. Similar to Dante, Jack Shephard finds himself in the "woods," "midway on life's journey," a life which, in a superficial sense, seems to be humming along just fine until the plane crash.

Abandon all hope, ye who enter here.

These words, familiar to even modern readers, are inscribed on the gates to hell in Dante's *Inferno*. There is no escape from this city and those who enter should consider their situation hopeless. A lack of faith, then, and a sense of utter despondency define the terms of this particular hell. Richard Alpert conveys a similar message to the other characters in the opening scene of "Ab Aeterno," as his faith quickly disintegrates upon the death of Jacob. So when he says "we are in hell" he is speaking the truth, in the sense that hell is a state of mind devoid of all hope. But not all is lost for either Dante or the castaways. A collective effort and a cultivation of faith will save them and elevate them to the point where they can "get back up to the shining world from there / My guide and I went into that hidden tunnel . . . / Where we came forth, and once more saw the stars." These points of light — *un*fallen stars — represent the source of life and a hope for the future (Alighieri 1900).

3

Who Has the "Power Over the Clay"? Purpose, Fate and Free Will

Every choice you've made in your life . . . it hasn't really been a choice at all, has it? It's in your nature. It's what you are.

— Benjamin Linus ("He's Our You")

Freedom is what you do with what's been done to you.

— Jean-Paul Sartre (1943)

The careful balance of free will and predetermination

Among other things, *Lost* is an allegorical study of the tension between fate and free will, questioning whether human beings control their own destinies or if other forces determine, or have already predetermined, the courses of their lives. In this chapter, I will explore this idea in the context of various works of literature and discuss the television series' attempt to maintain a balance between two competing philosophical constructs.

In simplistic terms, a debate about the concept of free will versus fatalism might go something like this: either there is a predestined purpose for each human being and there exists a meaningful order to the universe, or there is no cosmic plan, things happen arbitrarily and purpose is crafted by the individual alone. On the one hand, personal choices always affect outcome; on the other, something or someone exterior to the individual has planned the outcome with foreknowledge of each and every personal choice and its subsequent destination. It is noteworthy that the word destination has its origin in the term destiny, signifying that more than one language, including English, supports the idea that fate has a hand in any given journey or quest, the end point being a "destined-nation."

Many examples in *Lost*, most notably Desmond Hume's story, have offered viewers a fine balance of these two opposing concepts. Though at times it seems that Daniel Faraday's comments on the nature of time travel ("whatever happened, happened" but "any one of us can die") contradict one another, they actually provide an interesting and complex response to this philosophical puzzle, at least within the *Lost* universe. Using a combination of the complicated television narrative, and the messages implicit in the works of fiction reviewed in this book, I have constructed a working model for the notion of free will in *Lost*: There exists a general sketch of a cosmic plan for everything, what Stephen Hawking might call a "grand unifying" design (Hawking, *A Briefer History of Time* 2005). But this sketch is only a guide, like the outline of an essay; the individual parts are moveable and the details are malleable. There is a purpose in store for those who choose to embrace it and such a thing as a "best case" destiny. Individuals are responsible for their actions and decisions, but they are pushed in the right direction by outside forces.

Defining fate, destiny, predestination, determinism and free will

Before examining the various works of literature and their diverse messages about free will, it is important to review, if only superficially, a few of the significant theological and philosophical theories on this topic. The following passages serve to clarify the distinctions among the notion of determinism, a Calvinist conception of predestination and the broader definition of fatalism.

Determinism

Determinism, or more specifically causal determinism, is "the idea that every event is necessitated by antecedent events and conditions together with the laws of nature" ("Determinism" 2010). *Slaughterhouse-Five*'s protagonist Billy Pilgrim would likely agree with this notion, attesting that to proselytize this idea is to aid in the prevention of unnecessary human suffering that arises from the responsibility to alter one's reality. In contrast, *Lost*'s Jack Shephard is an example of someone who suffers greatly under the impression that he alone controls the shape of his life. He takes full responsibility for the direction of his own path (and sometimes the paths of others' lives). Determinism is "a philosophy that subordinates the importance of human choice and will to other forces that limit or even dictate human actions." Though there are limiting factors, there is no higher order or purposeful force at play (Childers and Hentzi 1995, 362).

Fatalism

Fatalism denotes a general understanding of the universe as dictated and preordained by an influence outside of human authority. It usually depends on the assumption that there exists a deity or omnipresent being that possesses foreknowledge or forethought of the future and the choices that each mortal will make, but it can be defined more generically, requiring only a general force that creates order for the universe. "Fatalism is the thesis that human acts occur by necessity and hence are unfree . . . [it] is easily disentangled from determinism, to the extent that one can disentangle mystical forces and gods' wills and foreknowledge [about specific matters] from the notion of natural/causal law" ("Fatalism" 2010).

"The Fates" of ancient mythology

The Fates of Greek and Roman mythology are depicted as three women who spin, measure and snip the threads of life. They personify destiny, determining the path of each human life and, as Hesiod claims, allotting portions of good and evil to each man at the time of his birth. The three are called the Moirae, or Moirai, in Greek mythology: "Clotho, the Spinner, who spun the thread of life; Lachesis, the Disposer of Lots, who assigned to each man his destiny; [and] Atropos . . . who carried 'the abhorred shears' and cut the thread at death" (Hamilton 1969, 49). Like the Moirae, Jacob spins the thread and then weaves the threads together, in the same way that he connects different lives to each other and to the island ("The Incident").

Predestination

This theological idea posits that an intelligent, all-knowing god has things planned out from the beginning of time for each mortal being. Predestination has been interpreted in many different respects, most literally by the Calvinists, but certainly not settled by biblical works. John Calvin told his followers that "God preordained . . . a part of the human race, without any merit of their own, to eternal salvation, and another part, in just punishment of their sin, to eternal damnation" (Calvin 2008). These are harsh words but notably applicable to those

Lost characters who seem to have less and less control over their destinies throughout the progression of the series.

The following biblical passage also supports the theory of predestination: "For whom he foreknew, he also predestined to become conformed to the image of his Son, that he might be the first-born among many brethren; and whom he predestined, these he also called; and whom he called, these he also justified; and whom he justified, these he also glorified" (Rom. 8.29–30). One of the works attributed to the apostle Paul, the Letter to the Ephesians, contains several references to God's fixed plan. In chapter 1, verse 11, Paul claims that "In him we were also chosen, destined in accord with the purpose of the One who accomplishes all things according to the intention of his will" (Eph. 1.11).

Free will and Christianity

> We all have our temptations, but giving in to them, that's your choice. As we live our lives it's really nothing but a series of choices, isn't it?
>
> — Charlie Pace's Priest in "The Moth"

A more widely embraced Christian interpretation of biblical texts supports the existence of free will. The works of St. Thomas Aquinas, for instance, promote the argument that a Christian god allows people to make their own choices. In the *Summa Theologica* Aquinas claims that people act according to their own judgment and free will: "otherwise counsels, exhortations, commands, prohibitions, rewards, and punishments would be in vain. . . . And forasmuch as man is rational it is necessary that man have a free-will" (Aquinas 1920).

Jacob, the mysterious island-dweller of *Lost*, brings people to the island for the sole purpose of proving to the Man in Black that humans can make the right decisions, even without the potential for an external reward. In "Ab Aeterno" when Richard asks Jacob why he doesn't help those who are brought to the island, Jacob provides a response akin to Aquinas's theory: "Because I wanted them to help themselves. To know the difference between right and wrong without me having to tell them. It's all meaningless if I have to force them to do anything. Why should I have to step in?"

Secular philosophy and free will

Rather than defining the secular conception of free will, I provide here an illustration of it in a literary text and present the ideas of the most influential of existentialists, Jean-Paul Sartre. Within the discussion of a Sartrean free will we should first visit a few notable passages by Fyodor Dostoevsky, a favorite *Lost* author, garnering more than one work on the list of the show's book cameos.

Sartre's literary and philosophical predecessor, Dostoevsky, offers compelling notions about free will in *Notes From Underground*, the novel that appears in season six of *Lost*, shortly after the death of Ilana. A passage relevant to our discussion here is articulated by the central character, the "man from underground." He declares, "One's own free and unfettered volition, one's own caprice, however wild, one's own fancy, inflamed sometimes to the point of madness — that is the one best and greatest good . . . What a man needs is simply and solely independent volition, whatever that independence may cost and wherever it may lead" (Dostoevsky 1972, 33). In *The Brothers Karamazov*, another novel featured in *Lost*,[1] Ivan Karamazov crafts a tale that he calls "The Grand Inquisitor." In this story-within-a-story the Grand Inquisitor dismisses the notion of free will as costly and impractical for the majority of people. He attacks Jesus Christ for defending it, saying, "for nothing has ever been so more insupportable for a man and a human society than freedom" (Dostoevsky, *The Brothers Karamazov* 1999, 245) Like the Man in Black in "The Incident," the Grand Inquisitor has little faith in the common person and supports the idea of controlling and caring for the masses. "They will understand at last that freedom and bread enough for all are inconceivable. Never, never will they be able to have both together! They will be convinced that they can never be free, for they are weak, vicious, worthless and rebellious" (246). Ultimately, this epic work suggests that free will, though problematic, is one of man's greatest powers. Sartre takes the notion further by explicitly declaring that human beings always have a choice and that the will of the individual is the only force that matters.

No Exit

In the early episodes of *Lost* there is great debate among the survivors as to whether the island and/or the Others have a plan and know why they are there. By the time the Others start talking about "The List," viewers understand that there is something of a plan in the works for the castaways. But it also becomes clear, as the story continues, that this plan might not be as foolproof, nor the Others as omniscient, as viewers initially assumed. This tension in the narrative of *Lost* is similar to the debate that develops among the characters of Jean-Paul Sartre's play *No Exit*.

The dramatic work illustrates well its famous quote, "Hell — is other people." First performed in 1943, it is said to be the fictitious expression of Sartre's great work of existentialism, *Being and Nothingness*. Three deceased souls, Inez, Estelle and Garcin, are stuck in a room for all of eternity. They have each earned their way into hell by making others suffer unnecessarily. Notably, the sins for which they are being punished are not broad in scale or remarkably evil. They arise from intimate relationships. This is not unlike the scope of transgressions that the *Lost* castaways must confront from their pre-island lives. *No Exit* poses questions about the nature of sin and suffering. Is the misery that we inflict on ourselves and others preordained or left to chance? Is there anything we can do about it, or is our nature created so that we have no choice but to cause each other suffering? How do our surroundings help us hurt each other in the way the furnishings of the room do for the trio of characters in Sartre's play? Ultimately, is there a grand scheme from which we can never escape, or do we construct prisons out of our own free will?

As Sandra Bonetto points out in her essay "No Exit From the Island: A Sartrean Analysis of *Lost*" the island is a "form of 'existentialist hell.' It centers on the conscious, lived experiences of its central characters who find themselves in a situation — akin to the absurd and meaningless universe that forms the existentialist backdrop to human existence — that has not been entered into freely and from which there appears to be no escape" (Bonetto 2008, 126). Since the beginning of the series, the island has been compared to the larger experience of life, not only by critics and fans attempting to construct an allegory of *Lost*, but also by the executive producers. Damon Lindelof claims that "[t]his show is about people who are metaphorically lost in their lives who get on an airplane and crash on an island and become physically lost on the planet Earth, and once they are able to metaphorically find themselves in their lives again, they will be able to physically find themselves in the world again" (Ryan 2007).

It is most helpful then to examine *No Exit* by way of Sartre's explicitly philosophical work, *Being and Nothingness*. Jean-Paul Sartre is remembered more for his ideas on existentialism than for his dramas.

In contrast to the ideas of passive fatalism that we have addressed thus far, as well as the "fine balance of fate and free will," Sartre believes that as conscious beings we are "wholly free" to choose our outcomes and that there is no path that is predetermined for us (Sartre, *Being and Nothingness* 1943). I will not attempt to conduct a sufficient analysis of even his most influential ideas here, but I should provide this basic Sartrean tenet: nothing is predestined and there is no truth in causal determinism or if there is determinism at all it is a self-determinism. Man alone controls his path in life and only death can turn a life into "destiny."

As the play begins, the three characters condemned to an eternity of each others' company are just letting go of their previous lives. They can see fleeting images of the people and places they have left behind, and each one overhears the comments that are uttered in their absence.

As they grapple with their preconceptions of hell, comparing it to the seemingly innocuous environment in which they find themselves, one notion that bothers all of them is whether or not there is a master plan conducting their damnation. Estelle says "isn't it better to think we got here by mistake?" Inez claims they were all put there together "deliberately." She seems to believe and expect that the other two are there to torture her. This suspicion, of course, as in any group dynamic in life, leads to trouble and the self-fulfilling prophecy of a torturous relationship. She suspects Garcin is her punisher and so he will become exactly that. He suspects the same of her, initiating a destructive cycle. It soon becomes apparent that their punishment does not require physical torture or fire and brimstone — they create hell for themselves. It drives Garcin to plead for physical torture saying, "anything would be better than this agony of mind, this creeping pain that gnaws and fumbles and caresses one and never hurts quite enough" (Sartre, *No Exit and Three Other Plays* 1976, 41).

At first, Garcin and Estelle believe that they have been put together by a "pure fluke," in which case they might have some control over their destinies. But Inez convinces them that they are there by design: "This room was all set for us," she says (14). Estelle eventually reveals evidence of her own fatalist attitude in life, when she shirks the guilt and blames an act of adultery on predestination. Six years into her marriage she "met the man [she] was fated to love" (16). Meanwhile Garcin begins to believe that "everything has been thought out beforehand" (45). Inez's comments reflect their growing paranoia of this preordained "snare" and suggest that the authorities (whoever they may be) have "foreknown every word" (30).

Against the backdrop of Sartre's idea that "there is no other destiny (for man) than the one he forges himself" the characters' fears seem like ridiculous, self-fulfilling prophecies. They illustrate Sartre's points clearly — we make our own heaven or hell — we are fully responsible and no outside force visits suffering upon us intentionally. Viewers may recall the Buddha-esque phrase flashed across the screen in Room 23 in the *Lost* episode of the same name: "We are the causes of our own suffering." By the end of the play it is clear to the audience that these three characters will "go round and round in a vicious circle" (30) torturing one another only because they believe they have no other choice. This notion illustrates how some *Lost* characters passively leave to fate events that they could control. "Don't mistake coincidence for fate," Eko warns John Locke, implying that John's passive fatalism will lead him astray ("What Kate Did").

The Wonderful Wizard of Oz

Various elements of L. Frank Baum's classic children's story pervade the narrative of the series: from hot air balloons to spiritual quests, to finding a way home, Dorothy's journey infuses *Lost* with its very particular imagery and compelling themes. The classic American tale is an ideal illustration of the tension between cosmic authority and individual motivation. Throughout the narrative there is an inter-weaving of both threads, but as we see the central protagonist grow emotionally, the strand of free will becomes stronger. In the beginning she sees herself as "only an ordinary little girl who had come by the chance of a cyclone into a strange land" (24), but by the end of the story she has overcome this sense of passivity and become a witting architect of her journey.

Let us presume that fate, as opposed to the notion of "chance," has a hand in Dorothy's house landing in Oz, initiating her journey and stoking the fires of conflict by killing the Wicked Witch of the East. Indeed, Dorothy does not intend for the house to fly about in the tor-nado and land in another world, and it is reasonable to suggest that if she had a choice in the matter, she would prefer that the house stay in Kansas, on the ground. What she does not realize is that this act of fate is pushing her toward her purpose.

Even after Dorothy arrives in Oz, she still does not have a sense of purpose; she knows only that she needs to find a way home. This primary, individual purpose will serve as a guide to help her find a broader, more spiritual purpose. Her journey will provide the tools and knowledge she needs in order to assert her free will. As she travels through the magical land of Oz, she asserts her free will time and again, while being periodically guided by acts of fate.

Unlike the film adaptation, in which Glinda the Good magically places the ruby slippers on Dorothy's feet, in the novel, Dorothy *chooses* to don the witch's silver shoes. After the witch's body instantaneously turns to dust, Glinda offers the shoes to Dorothy, saying, "there is some charm connected with them; but what it is we never knew" (Baum 2008, ch. 2). Dorothy does not put them on right away and when she does, it is her choice alone to wear the shoes and, thus, enter into the world of mystery and accept the challenge of the quest. But when she does, she also discovers that they must be destined for her feet.[2] "She took off her old leather shoes and tried on the silver ones, which fitted her as well as if they had been made for her" (Baum 2008, ch. 3). An act of free will leads to a fated purpose.

As Dorothy continues her journey she meets other individuals, each with a purpose of his own. The Scarecrow needs a brain (intellect and reason), the Tin Woodman needs a heart (love, compassion) and the Lion is seeking courage. They all share in common the belief that their destination, Oz, will fulfill their purpose. Until their journeys are complete, they are unable to see that their experiences and their own choices play a significant role in their outcomes.

On the first of three journeys that make up this quest story, Dorothy, the Tin Woodman, the Scarecrow and the Cowardly Lion all band together to find the great and "terrible" wizard. Their expedition has been interpreted in many different ways — a quest for one's soul, a search for God, a call to justice. Although this story has been widely construed as an allegory about industrialization and its effect on the agrarian culture, for the sake of this discussion I will simply view it as a spiritual quest, similar to the journeys of the *Lost* characters.

In this sense, Dorothy follows her yellow brick road to find a powerless and impotent god. The promise of finding a magical resolution to her conflict is not fulfilled, but the "humbug" wizard does succeed in revealing the travelers' true gifts. With his help, Dorothy and her companions discover that their journey, more than anything else, has imbued them with the gifts they were seeking. Most *Lost* fans will recognize that this principle — placing value in the journey itself over the outcome of the quest — is common to both *The Wonderful Wizard of Oz* and the narrative of *Lost*.

Dorothy begins to realize that the wizard, a god-like figure of power at the beginning, is reduced to just another victim of fate himself. By learning that he is not all-knowing and all-seeing, she gains confidence in her own decisions and realizes her freedom to choose her own path. The same is true of her friends, the Scarecrow, the Tin Woodman and the Lion — they want to believe in a great and powerful being and a controller of fate — but once they realize that they themselves construct their own gifts (love, intellect and courage), they are able to shape their destinies.

But before this resolution comes into play, Dorothy finds that her purpose in Oz extends to an entire people. Like the *Lost* castaways, she is flung into a strange world unwillingly, where her own hero's journey[3] is set into motion. The Great and Powerful Oz assigns her the task of destroying the last Wicked Witch of the land and saving all inhabitants from terror. Like John Locke when Ben asks him to kill Anthony Cooper, Dorothy is hesitant. She responds, "I never killed anything, willingly . . . Even if I wanted to, how could I kill the Wicked Witch? If you, who are Great and Terrible, cannot kill her yourself, how do you expect me to do it?" This is a classic question posed by any hero: "Why me?" This moment of reluctance and self-reflection transforms the common traveler into a hero.

The witch, of course, acts as a god of Fate. Her constituency and sorcery bear more than a passing resemblance to the Others and their technological wizardry. When Dorothy sets out on a quest to destroy the witch, the little girl becomes a subject of surveillance. The witch, a sort of demi-god and, therefore, a helping hand of fate, demonstrates her powers of omniscience. The round television screens of the Dharma barracks, that provide powers of omniscience to the Dharma folks and the Others, resemble the witch's crystal ball in the film. In the book, the witch has only one eye, a telescopic eye that can "see everywhere" (Baum 2008, ch. 10). Imbued with the ability to "see all," the Others are able to manipulate the castaways to follow their grand scheme. (Later in the series this capacity for omniscience is reflected in Jacob and the Man in Black, or the Smoke Monster.) Similarly, the witch alters the path of Dorothy and her friends.

Although she gains the ability to act upon her own free will, Dorothy is never completely reliant on her own resources and choices. Her success is always dependent on what some might call coincidence. (Indeed, here I am deliberately "mistaking" coincidence for fate, as Eko accuses John of doing in "What Kate Did.") Her act of killing the second witch, the Wicked Witch of the West, is the result of an angry outburst, not a premeditated design. The water she throws at the witch can be construed as a fateful provision. The "spinners of Fate" put it there for her. In the same way, with an all-powerful kiss, Glinda the Good protects Dorothy throughout her journey. It leaves a mark that strikes fear in both the Winged Monkey and the Wicked Witch of the West. Glinda's god-like status allows her to control Dorothy's fate by shielding her from harm.

Dorothy and friends are guided by the gods of their world (the witches) just as the castaways' paths are shaped by the forces of the island (Others, Jacob, the Smoke Monster). But they also assert their free will, sometimes surprising the "gods of fate," those who see themselves as implementers of the plan.

Slaughterhouse-Five

Only on earth is there any talk of free will.
— A Tralfamadorian, *Slaughterhouse-Five*
(Vonnegut 1969, 109)

The central figure in Kurt Vonnegut's cult classic *Slaughterhouse-Five* is not a typical hero; in fact he has been described as an anti-hero in an anti-novel. But his passivity and open mind make Billy Pilgrim a prime receptor of the philosophy of the Tralfamadorians, an advanced race of aliens, creatures who can foresee the end of time. Struggling to understand the Tralfamadorians' conception of fate, Billy wants to know why the button-pusher who destroys the universe would continue to push the button even with the knowledge of such a tragic outcome. Why doesn't he stop himself? A Tralfamadorian explains, "He has *always* pressed it, and he *always* will. We *always* let him and we *always* will let him. The moment is *structured* that way." Here, the reader is introduced to the deterministic perspective that Billy will adopt and begin preaching to the rest of humanity. His motive to spread this idea is to provide comfort among his fellow Earth dwellers. He wants people to know that they suffer because they feel in control when they really are not. They suffer because they blame themselves for their circumstances, not realizing that this is the way things are and will always be, regardless of individual effort or choice. Viewers of *Lost* might recall the phrase, "We are the causes of our own suffering," featured in the brainwashing Dharma film in "Room 23."

Slaughterhouse-Five is a model of non-linear storytelling, a jumble of scenes viewed through the eyes of Billy, a confused subject of time travel, trying to work through the tragedy he witnessed in Dresden as a young man. Vonnegut's choice to use time travel in an anti-war novel is not arbitrary. In fact, the sudden temporal shifts have everything to do with the nature of Billy's post-traumatic stress and his role in the war, illustrating an explosion of his timeline, with pieces falling here and there, all mixed up. The firebombing of Dresden is a key image for reading the exploded timeline of Billy's life. This same narrative device is used in *Lost*. Billy's time-jumping is similar to what happens after Desmond turns the failsafe key ("Live Together, Die Alone") and uncontrollably travels to various points in his past. The viewers experience the effects of the hatch explosion through a disorienting eruption of the narrative timeline. This mechanism aids in expressing the inexplicable (war) and illustrating the interior struggle of one character.

The novel itself is a device to help Vonnegut, a World War II veteran, work through his own personal postwar devastation. He creates a significant amount of distance from the war by providing two layers of perspective. The first and last chapters of the book are told in first-person point of view by an unnamed veteran of World War II. Presumably the same narrator tells the rest of the story but it is all through Billy Pilgrim's perspective, with the narrator privy to Billy's thoughts.

Billy is decidedly *not* Vonnegut's alter ego. Where Billy is resigned to a life of passive fatalism, Vonnegut's message, if there is a single message, is much more complex. In general, Vonnegut seems to assert that even if the notion of having power over our destinies is only an illusion, we should still be able to exercise our freedom to act. "The basic quality he wishes to preserve in humanity is our ability to live *as if* we have free will" (Thomas 2006, 24). Where Vonnegut might embrace the creed set forth in the "Serenity Prayer," Billy believes that "among the things [he] could not change were the past, the present, and the future" (Vonnegut 1969, 77). The serenity prayer, written by American Christian theologian Reinhold Neibhur, is prominently displayed in a frame in Billy's office (76). "God, give us grace to accept with serenity the things that cannot be changed, courage to change the things that can be changed, and the wisdom to distinguish one from the other."

The bombing of Dresden and the senselessness of war lie at the center of this work; thus, the most notable time to which Billy travels is 1945. The place, of course, is a war-torn Europe. The first occurrence of Billy becoming "unstuck in time" is his leap from age 46 to age 18 at the end of World War II. Like Desmond, only his consciousness travels through time, though some critics would argue that the notion of time travel in *Slaughterhouse-Five*, as well as the other science-fiction elements, is merely a symptom of mental illness.[4]

In *Lost*, as Desmond travels through time and meets Eloise Hawking, he begins to realize that his actions have little influence on fate. He can delay Charlie's death but he cannot altogether prevent it from happening. In accordance with the working model established at the beginning of this chapter, the plan is already sketched out and the outcome non-negotiable, but the details are flexible. Billy Pilgrim, however, does not challenge fate or even try to alter the minor events. He knows that he will be the only survivor of a plane wreck and he knows how his wife will die, but he never tries to alter these tragic events. He is a passive fatalist, just as Desmond becomes after trying to protect Charlie several times. Ultimately he knows that Charlie will die, whether from a bolt of lightning, a snare in the jungle or by drowning.

"You're gonna die, Charlie," warns Desmond. On the one hand, this statement is not particularly profound: we all know that we are "gonna die" sooner or later. But perhaps the variable or malleable details really do matter. As Jacob claims, "it only ends once. Anything that happens up until then is just progress" ("The Incident"). This brief philosophical exchange that he shares with the Man in Black on the beach recalls *Slaughterhouse-Five*'s first-person narrator, presumably Kurt Vonnegut himself, who says: "There will always be wars." In the context of Vonnegut's overall message (war is hellish and senseless), this statement can be interpreted as a call to action: though humans are bound to a certain collective destiny which destroys and corrupts, they can still implement change, however small the effort seems compared to the colossal forces at play. The novel reveals the absolute absurdity of war, urging its readers to delay combat and diminish violent conflict, just as Desmond takes what control he can over Charlie's destiny. Overall, *Lost* suggests that humans are ultimately responsible for one another and should be all the more vigilant in knowing that "They come. They fight. They destroy. They corrupt. It always ends the same" ("The Incident").

Lost Horizon

James Hilton's novel, *Lost Horizon*, has more in common with the narrative of *Lost* than any other work of fiction mentioned in this book. Although the two stories are not identical, by any means, they share enough narrative devices and thematic nodes to make such a strong claim of commonality.

First published in 1933, the novel is set in a fictitious region in China during a period of political conflict. Like *Lost*, it begins realistically, setting the characters in a world with which the readers are familiar. No evidence of the supernatural reveals itself until more than halfway through the text. Certainly *Lost* presents the Smoke Monster in the very first episode, but viewers presume it can be explained rationally, just like the "coincidences" of Hilton's novel can initially be understood in the context of the known world.

The novel's main protagonist, Conway or "Glory" Conway, is a British ambassador working in the Baskul region when a fierce rebellion erupts among the local people. Conway is charged with evacuating all foreigners out of the country, or as the text bluntly reports, "Air Force machines arrived by arrangement from Peshawar to evacuate all of the white residents" (Hilton 1960, 20). When he is finally able to leave, he boards a plane with the last three evacuees — Mallinson, a young British man, Barnard a successful, if corrupt, American businessman-turned-fugitive, and Miss Brinklow, a Christian missionary. As the flight progresses, they notice that the plane is off course, heading toward uncharted Himalayan territory. After a day and night of flying, the plane crashes near a Tibetan lamasery. Shortly before dying, their hijacker reveals to the four passengers the extent to which the plane traveled off course.

The survivors, seemingly stranded in desolate tundra, are soon rescued by the members of the lamasery and brought to Shangri-La, a utopian community set in a lush Eden-like valley, where they stay for months afterward. Conway, like *Lost*'s John Locke, embraces the new life offered by the mysterious dwelling. He immediately feels a spiritual connection and ultimately finds his cosmic purpose in the monastery, in much the same way that select characters in *Lost* find their calling as "candidates" to replace Jacob. Conway also learns that the residents enjoy extended lives and that the valley has healing and restorative powers.[5] The High Lama reveals to him that they were brought there for a particular purpose; all of the residents who come are chosen. Their hijacker, in other words, was ordered to bring each one of them to Shangri-La *for a reason*.[6] The High Lama, who has his *Lost* counterpart in Jacob, serves as a clear illustration of the balance between free will and fate, especially when he reveals that although the attempt to bring Conway to Shangri-La was planned and intentional, it also depended on many variables falling into place. The High Lama, aware of his impending death, needed a replacement and fate played a part in Conway's arrival.

Mallinson, on the other hand, is eager to leave and doubtful of the High Lama's intentions. He grows increasingly impatient and fearful, suspecting that the community and the monks harbor malevolent plans for the castaways. Shangri-La's enchantment seems dangerous and Mallinson's single goal becomes to "escape" by any means. Quite simply, he is a predecessor to *Lost*'s character, Jack Shephard.

As the party first makes their ascent to Shangri-La, Conway and Mallinson discuss their circumstances. The younger man wants to know why Conway is unperturbed by the terrifying hijacking incident and the mysterious reception of the high priest and his people. "You're too confounded philosophic for me," Mallinson accuses Conway. "That wasn't your mood at Baskul." The older man's reply is reminiscent of John Locke at his most inspired: "Of course not, because there I could alter events with my own actions. But now, for the moment at least, there's no such chance. We're here because we're here, if you want a reason." This statement reveals Conway's ability to act when necessary but to accept what fate has in store. His outlook is pragmatic but he knows there is a reason he can't take action; it is time for destiny to act upon him. He is learning to uphold the delicate balance of the universe. In *Lost*, John Locke never seems to achieve this same kind of balance, but the pairing of Jack and Locke sometimes promises that equilibrium.

Mallinson finally convinces Conway to leave with him. But once Conway returns to "civilization" he immediately embarks on a journey to find Shangri-La once again. This reveals the final and most significant similarity between *Lost Horizon* and *Lost*: the ending of the novel is left open to the audience's interpretation. It is never established if Mallinson was right to doubt the High Lama's intentions. And we never learn about the outcome of Conway's journey. Does he make it back to Shangri-La? In many respects *Lost* also ends ambiguously; perhaps the legacy of *Lost* will be characterized by continued reinterpretation.

Fate and the afterlife

The final work that I touch upon in this chapter occupies itself not so much with life's mysterious journey, but the fate of souls in the afterlife. Like *No Exit*, it serves to examine hell as an allegory for life. They both reflect the sense of an existential hell, the notion that the cyclical nature of ordinary life provides punishment enough for those who continue to revisit their sins. According to Joe, a spirit figure in *The Third Policeman*, "Hell goes round and round. In shape it is circular and by nature it is interminable, repetitive and very nearly unbearable"

(O'Brien 1967, 200). In failing to redeem themselves, these characters create for themselves an island, an underworld where they are isolated from others and, in a very Christian sense, separated from God.

The Third Policeman

> Humanity is an ever-widening spiral and life is the beam that plays briefly on each succeeding ring. All humanity from its beginning to its end is already present but the beam has not yet played beyond you.
>
> — O'Brien (1967, 119)

Flann O'Brien's "black comedy" was posthumously published in 1967, but he references the work in a letter to Andy Gillett in 1940, explaining the original qualities of his developing narrative. The unnamed narrator and central character has "recourse to the local barrack which, however, contains some very extraordinary policemen who do not confine their investigations or activities to this world or to any known planes or dimensions. Their most casual remarks create a thousand other mysteries . . . The whole point of my plan will be the most brain-staggering imponderables of the policeman" (Asbee 1991). If we substitute the word "policemen" for "Others," this comment could easily be attributed to the writers of *Lost* who seem to delight in creating "a thousand other mysteries," on top of the thousands of questions already posed, and "the most brain-staggering imponderables" that continue to puzzle viewers.

Beyond the perspective of the writers, there are numerous similarities between *Lost* and *The Third Policeman*, as others have pointed out already.[7] In both stories, there are underground bunkers where the numbers or "readings" preoccupy the characters' daily lives; they fear that an explosion or catastrophe might occur if these duties are neglected. In *The Third Policeman*, there is a cabinet that produces anything the wisher desires, much like the "box" that Ben promises will respond to John's wishes. Further, both the novel and the television program feature maps prominently displayed on the ceilings of their bunkers. In O'Brien's story, a map of eternity can be seen in the cracks of the ceilings and in *Lost* John Locke finds a cryptic map written on the blast door ("Lockdown"). In season six, Sawyer discovers a map of sorts, a mosaic of names and numbers, which serves as a key to the mystery of Jacob's chosen "candidates," scrawled on the ceiling of the cave.

The plot of the novel, however, as well as the tone, is very different from the adventure/sci-fi/mystery/thriller television series. It is fantastic in nature but, more than anything, a metaphysical satire. The unnamed narrator of *The Third Policeman* commits murder while robbing a man for money to fund his research project, a work he calls the "De Selby Index." The murder of Mathers, in which the narrator plays a brutal part, is a cold-blooded killing, according to Jeffrey Mathewes, author of "The Manichaean Body in *The Third Policeman*: or Why Joe's Skin Is Scaly" (Mathewes n.d.). Here he describes why the scene is so disturbing. "On the one hand, O'Nolan's [O'Brien's real name] imagery highlights the fragility of human life at the same time that it wallows in the vileness of the gruesome details of its destruction. On the other hand, he describes the narrator's movements as mechanical. Like a machine or puppet, the narrator acts mechanically, like a dispassionate tool of unseen forces when he takes Mathers' life" (Mathewes 9).

The narrator himself is also murdered, by his partner in crime, and most of the novel takes place in an "interminable . . . and very nearly unbearable" (O'Brien 1967, 200) afterlife in which two policemen help him navigate this strange new world. The catch is that he has no awareness of his own death. Neither do the readers know that he is dead until the end of the book, at which time the narrator understands only for a moment the nature of his condition. His memory is then wiped clean and he proceeds to repeat the same story, doomed for eternity to relive his suffering and repeat the same mistakes. Unlike many of *Lost*'s central characters, he will not be able to "move on."

The Third Policeman's vision of the afterlife demonstrates that there is no escape from our existence; not even in death will we be able to fully understand or gain perspective on the human condition. Naively, the narrator says, "Down into the earth where dead men go I would go soon and maybe come out of it again in some healthy way, free and innocent of all human perplexity." Sue Asbee uses this quote to illustrate the true nature of the narrator's predicament — he will never be free — and the reader sympathizes with this notion, especially when reading the novel a second time around. "The implications for this sympathy are chilling, for when we reread, we are sharply aware that, as far as this novel is concerned, freedom, innocence and understanding are forever beyond human reach. The narrator has actually become immortal, but he is unaware of the fact and will never be in a position to understand, because he is beyond redemption" (Asbee 1991).

As the narrator contemplates his own death, he hears the voice of Joe. Up until this point "Joe" seems like a separate entity, some sort of spirit floating in or around the narrator. Here, he reveals not only his identity, but the nature of human existence and how one constructs the other. "Listen," says Joe. "Before I go I will tell you this. I am your soul and all your souls. When I am gone you are dead. Past humanity is not only implicit in each new man born but is contained in him" (119). This idea provides clues to what is happening on the island. As Daniel Faraday claims, you can't change the past because everything is "already present."

Balancing fate and free will in *Lost*

Although Jacob and the Smoke Monster, forces that represent god-like authority, seem to have powers of omniscience at times, they rely on the individual to do what he is "supposed to do" which only he alone knows how to do. In "The Economist" (4.3), Sawyer asks Locke how he survived Benjamin Linus's gunshot. He responds by revealing the bullet wound, explaining that if he still had his kidney, the shot would have killed him. Viewers will recall Ben's first murder attempt: before he leaves Locke for dead in the pit of Dharma corpses, he says, "I hope Jacob can help you now, John." As destiny would have it, Anthony Cooper, recipient of Locke's kidney, turns out to be the savior in this fateful predicament. But it was John who made the decision to donate his kidney in the first place. Though he was duped, the choice he made was one that ultimately saved his own life. It was his own gullibility, but also his trustworthy nature, that saved him.

It is not until season three and Eloise Hawking's description of course correction that viewers begin to comprehend the show's tension between fate and free will: an individual's efforts to change the future may have short-term effects, but in the long run she will end up at her predestined location. Course correction is the single-most useful notion to help us understand the balance between free will and predetermination for the "Lostaways." To put it simply, the characters (and, presumably, the rest of us) are each destined to travel from point A to point B, no matter what. They can't change the fundamental course. The individual choices they make may cause them to stray from their original path, but eventually they will arrive at point B. However, they have the sense of being in control of their lives and their efforts to thwart fate can temporarily alter the path.

Lost: the fate of the story and the will of the writers

Even novelists must respect the balance between the creator's will and the individuality of each character. They sketch out the fictional world and an idea of the overall storyline, maybe even knowing the final outcome from the beginning. They are the creators, the gods of their narratives, so to speak. But as each story progresses, novelists must listen to their characters to determine what *they* would do in any given situation. The characters develop according to a given set of characteristics, and sometimes find different paths (than their author first intended) to their proscribed "destined-nation." If a novelist is too heavy-handed, the readers will feel that the events, motives and dialogue are overly contrived. The same phenomenon can be seen in the creative development of *Lost*.

Damon Lindelof has told viewers that from the beginning they knew the overarching scheme of the story, but that they worked out the details as they went, allowing Henry Gale, for instance, to become the Leader of the Others even though that particular bit was not in the original plan. So one might ask "Has not the potter power over the clay . . .?" (Rom. 9.21). But to say that the television writer does not have complete control over his creation is an understatement, considering that they, the "potters" of the story, must rely on the availability of the actors and actresses, the collaborative nature of television writing, the influence of fan reaction and, most notably, the approval of the network executives. With all of these forces at play, the creative process is likened to the journey of life, which is at the mercy of a multitude of influences, not the least of which is economic.

In an interview (Keveney 2010), executive co-producers Damon Lindelof and Carlton Cuse commented on the unpredictability of the writing process. Lindelof explained that they would write or oversee an episode and send it to Hawaii for production. Many times they would be surprised at the finished product. "You have this idea in your head of what (an episode) is going to be . . . and then it comes back (from production) and it's this entirely different thing." Such is the nature of collaborative storytelling, especially when it comes to television narratives, but even solitary novelists experience a similar feeling. Even from idea to drawing board the nature of the story will be modified and will continue to change until it is finished and released for readers or viewers. "It sounds so corny and so disingenuous but it's really true: the show has been telling us what it wants to be for quite some time now and we feel like we've been listening to it." Cuse added, "We were enriched by what we learned as we delved into these characters," implying that their own creations were showing them the way, rather than the other way around (Keveney 2010).

The notion of being "pushed" by fate is something I take directly from the show's dialogue. In episode four of season six, Locke explains to Sawyer that Jacob has provided the appropriate nudges to each chosen castaway in order to get him or her to the island. In season five Jacob mysteriously appears in Jack and Christian's hospital. Handing a candy bar to Jack he tells him, "It just needed a little push," referring to the Apollo Bar stuck in a vending machine but with the implication that a "push" is exactly what Jack needs ("The Incident"). Like the traveling companions in Baum's *The Wonderful Wizard of Oz*, writers must discover their purpose as they create it (or they must create as they discover) and then recognize that sometimes the journey matters more than the destination. Like Conway in James Hilton's *Lost Horizon*, individuals must know when to act and when to be acted upon. The universe might be able to "course correct," but not without the decisions that are made through the power of self-determination. The works of fiction presented above illustrate a wide range of perspectives on the notion of free will. Taken together, they support the theory that individual plans and motives act within a wider cosmic plan to create a complex depiction of history and destiny. Individuals work in concert with the universe to create what some call "fate."

4

Stuck and "Unstuck" in Time: A Tradition of Time Travel

In "Lost in Genre: Chasing the White Rabbit to Find a White Polar Bear" Angela Ndalianis presents the various narrative traditions from which *Lost* draws its character types, narrative devices and themes. This fusion of genres includes survivor stories, interpersonal dramas, the apocalyptic narrative, supernatural, horror and fantasy conventions and, of course, the science-fiction tradition (Ndalianis 2009). The genre-bending in which *Lost* engages is typical of recent televisual narratives demonstrated in such shows as *Fringe, Heroes* and *Flashforward*. According to Ndalianis this is not so much a creative decision as a result of corporate interests: implementing a multiplicity of genres casts a wider net and draws in more viewers, resulting in higher ratings. She points out that an interview with writer and producer David Fury reveals that "the ABC network, in particular, made clear its aversion to the *Lost* writers' stabilizing the series' genre affiliation — in particular with science fiction" (Ndalianis 2009). Indeed, *Lost* has been successful in maintaining its science-fiction fan base while attracting a wider mainstream audience, but its generic roots remain evident.

The series emerges from a science-fiction heritage that regularly employs the following conventions: radical technological experiments, unfamiliar or alien life forms, morally problematic psychological or medical experimentation, and the manipulation of the space–time continuum. This last narrative device, especially, places *Lost* squarely within the realm of the science-fiction tradition, but its introduction to the series may have alienated viewers unfamiliar or uncomfortable with this particular construct. It presents confusing potentialities within an already complicated plot that relies on non-linear storytelling. Akin to the prolepsis and analepsis (flashforward and flashback), time travel is used as a narrative device but plays a more complex role with the potential for characters to change history. To further complicate things, season six introduces a new perspective of the story with the possibility of an alternate timeline, what came to be known as the "flash sideways" scene but was ultimately exposed as a spiritual afterlife. This chapter addresses *Lost*'s position within the tradition of time travel narratives, focusing on various science-fiction precursors to the show. I will also approach the manipulation of the space–time continuum as a metaphor; this concept is of potential interest to a wider spectrum of viewers, as it addresses significant aspects of the human psyche.[1]

"A brief history of time" travel

Robert Silverberg, editor of *The Mirror of Infinity: A Critics' Anthology of Science Fiction*, notes that the literary form of science fiction finds its roots in the work of Lucian of Samosata in AD 2, whose lunar voyage story is considered to be the earliest known fantasy narrative with science-fiction elements. He also cites More's *Utopia* and Cyrano de Bergerac's *A Voyage to the Moon* as predecessors to the genre, and I would add Mary Shelley's *Frankenstein* to that list.

Another very early tale that conveys an impression of science-fiction mystery revolves around the notion of accelerated time. *Urashima Taro* is the story of a young fisherman summoned to the bottom of the ocean by a great Sea Emperor. There, the man finds an enchanted world where he spends the next three days; but when he resurfaces he discovers that hundreds of years have passed — all of his friends and family are long dead. This eighth-century Japanese fairy tale, though not based on scientific presumptions, is akin to time-travel narratives. It explores the implications of a rapid progression of time and the bleak glimpse into the future, far beyond the main character's life.

But it is the time-travel adventure stories of H. G. Wells that stand as clear predecessors of narratives like *Lost*. "Wells is the true father of today's science fiction," claims Silverberg, "for it was he who set the canons and techniques that most contemporary writers follow. [He] systematically conceived and explored each of the major themes of modern science fiction: the conflict between worlds, the social consequences of great inventions, the voyage in time, the possibility of the world's destruction" (Silverberg 1970, viii). Although *Lost* has been influenced by a multitude of stories and genres, it undoubtedly has a wide stripe of Wellsian science fiction running through it.

Modes of travel: Wells versus Vonnegut

Lost employs two different types of time travel: corporeal, in which the traveler uses a portal or technological device to physically move through space and time (a reflection of the Wells concept), and the form that resembles Billy Pilgrim's movement of consciousness through time in Kurt Vonnegut's *Slaughterhouse-Five*. The former plays out in season five when the island and most, if not all, of its inhabitants travel through time. The latter is demonstrated in Desmond's experience ("The Constant"), Daniel Faraday's experimentations and George Minkowski's tragic death.

The Time Machine

John Locke: "Hey. Uh . . . was he talking about what I think he was talking about?"

Ben: "If you mean time-travelling bunnies, then yes."

— *Lost* season four finale, "There's No Place Like Home, Part 2"

In the season four finale episode, John Locke watches as Dr. Edgar Halliwax (also known as Pierre Chang) explains time travel in the Orchid Orientation video; in the same room Ben is frantically gathering metallic objects into a vault, a space that evidently has the capacity to transport its occupants through time. As Ben rushes around, Dr. Halliwax explains that a Casimir effect, created by the island's "unique properties," may be responsible for the Dharma Initiative's ability to conduct time-travel experiments. Halliwax places a white rabbit in the vault and closes the door, explaining that the subject will be transported 100 milliseconds into the future. The idea depicted in this orientation video, and the other explanations of time travel in *Lost*, borrow from one of the most famous time-travel stories of all time: *The Time Machine* by H. G. Wells.

First published in 1895, this story's notion of time travel is the forerunner to all modern time-travel stories. A man simply named "the Time Traveller" conducts experiments in time using a machine of his own creation. At dinner one evening, when his companions object to the feasibility of traveling through time, he compares the manipulation of the space–time continuum to the human memory. "But you are wrong to say that we cannot move about in Time. For instance, if I recall a moment very vividly, I go back to the instance of occurrence: I become absent-minded, as you say. I jump back for a moment" (Wells, *The Time Machine* 5). The Time Traveller compares potential innovations in time travel to inventions that defy gravity, such as the hot-air balloon. If man can travel through space by way of technological advancement, argues the Time Traveller, then why not "stop or accelerate his drift along the Time Dimension, or even turn about and travel the other way?" (5). He explains the fourth dimension as time, portraying space–time as a cube. "There are really four dimensions, three which we call the three planes of Space, and a fourth, Time. There is, however, a tendency to draw an unreal distinction between the former three dimensions and the latter, because it happens that our consciousness moves intermittently in one direction along the latter from the beginning to the end of our lives" (2). In *Lost*'s Dharma video, Dr. Halliwax uses this same model to explain the idea of time travel. The concept is no longer relevant to modern physics, but the author's description of it in *The Time Machine* has had a profound effect on the tradition of science-fiction notions of time, including *Lost*'s time-traveling island.[2]

Slaughterhouse-Five

> "It's a poor sort of memory that only works backwards," the
> Queen remarked.
> — The White Queen, *Through the Looking-Glass*
> *and What Alice Found There*

In Lewis Carroll's *Through the Looking-Glass and What Alice Found There* the White Queen says she "lives backwards" and that her memory works "both ways" (Carroll 2002). Understandably, little Alice is confused by this notion, but it might help viewers of *Lost* to understand what it would mean to have a memory that goes in both directions, one that could perceive everything from the beginning to the end of time, or, as some see it, the entire loop of time. In *Slaughterhouse-Five* Kurt Vonnegut uses the Tralfamadorians to help readers understand this perspective of time. They see all of time like a mountain range — they are equipped to look in all directions, whereas humans are limited to perceiving time through only one small forward-facing peephole.

Kurt Vonnegut's celebrated novel famously begins, "Listen: Billy Pilgrim has become unstuck in time." Pilgrim, a middle-aged widower travels to significant moments in his past, where he is thrown into the exact times and locations of his younger self. The Tralfamadorians, Billy's alien captors, perceive that most humans are like bugs trapped in amber, always stuck in the present moment. But Billy, a Tralfamadorian experiment, unwittingly moves around in space and time. This phenomenon is similar to the first references to time travel in *Lost* — the death of George Minkowski, Desmond's "flashes" and Daniel Faraday's lab experiments at Oxford with Eloise the mouse. These temporal changes apply only to the individual consciousness and are not apparent to anyone else; no one besides the traveler notices his departures and arrivals.

Using an analogy, the Tralfamadorians explain to Billy Pilgrim how they think humans perceive time. They see the human head as "encased in a steel sphere" with only one eyehole. Attached to this hole there is a six-foot tube of pipe. Humans can't turn their heads in any other direction — they can only see through the small round lens at the end of the pipe. Additionally, they are strapped to a vehicle that moves in only one direction on a metal track. But Billy is the exception. The aliens bestow on him a power that allows him to share their perspective; his consciousness travels through time, though he cannot control the movement. He re-experiences various points in his life, including his own birth and death. But the emphasis of the book is on his experiences in a war-torn Dresden: "with his memory of the future he knew the city would be smashed to smithereens and then burned in about thirty more days" (192).

Altering the past: more stories that prefigure the time-traveling island

In *The Time Machine* the central character travels far into the future, witnessing the end of humanity and disintegration of the world. This story and *Slaughterhouse-Five*, as well as the others presented in this chapter, are part of a narrative tradition within the realm of science fiction. Time-travel stories are governed by a set of implied rules, many established by Wells himself and some that are influenced by Einstein's theories and the progression of scientific advancements through the twentieth century. Lewis Carroll's Alice stories, though published not long before the time of H. G. Wells, are part of a different era and genre, but they nevertheless deal with the same conundrums of time and perception.

Allusions to the Alice stories have become commonplace in narratives of every genre, especially science fiction. In recent years the *Matrix* trilogy is the most notable example of this phenomenon; the film's reference to the rabbit hole and the chessboard imagery, as well as the notion that things are not always what they seem, make for a strong connection to Carroll's stories. But in the following short story, the author Asimov takes advantage of another motif for the title of his short story: the perception of time (though the central concern of the story is man's ability to alter the past).

Isaac Asimov: "The Red Queen's Race"

Now, here, you see, it takes all the running you can do, to keep in the same place. If you want to get somewhere else, you must run at least twice as fast as that!

— The Red Queen, *Through the Looking-Glass and What Alice Found There*

Written by celebrated science-fiction author Isaac Asimov, the short story "The Red Queen's Race" addresses a common theme of many time-travel narratives — the risk of permanently changing past events. The investigation of Elmer Tywood's physics experiment and subsequent death leads to a mystifying discovery. For supposedly altruistic purposes, Tywood constructs a system that would allow objects to travel through time, back to the Hellenistic Age. He wants to share modern-day scientific and technological advances with the ancient world, hoping it will change history for the better by eradicating widespread ignorance, the negative influences of the Church and the institution of slavery. His method of transmission is successful, but he requires a translator to effectively communicate the information. This translator, Professor Boulder, pretends to help him, but actually only prepares "such passages as would account for the queer scraps of knowledge the ancients apparently got from nowhere" (Asimov 1972, 498).

Tywood is already dead when the story begins and there is an investigation under way to determine not only the cause of death but the nature of his meddling in the time–space continuum. As the reader learns at the end of the story, Professor Tywood does not alter history after all; the translator makes sure of that by providing only "scraps." He tells the investigators "And my only intention, for all my racing, was to stay in the same place." The investigators conclude that Professor Boulder "could not be considered a criminal without being considered a world savior as well" (498). Boulder makes sure that history remains intact, fearing there could be devastating consequences otherwise. What he reveals is a sense of futility about the business of survival; for most people in this world the only reward for all of the hard labor and tedious work is merely staying alive. The good deeds only balance out the bad deeds, but will never overcome evil; similarly, the intelligent and insightful simply counteract the actions of the reckless and the stupid.

Ray Bradbury: "A Sound of Thunder"

This short work by Ray Bradbury, first published in 1952 and recently adapted into a film, tells the story of a time-travel company that offers safaris to far-off times and places. The central character, Eckels, has spent a good deal of money on a trip to prehistoric times where he is given the opportunity to hunt and kill a Tyrannosaurus Rex. The accompanying staff warn Eckels not to stray from the metal path or interact with the environment in any way. The dinosaur that Eckels plans to shoot has been preselected and marked with a red "X." The company has chosen this particular creature because they know the exact hour of its death; this ensures that the hunters don't alter history by intervening in the established design.

Evidently, the whole idea of time travel as leisure is a new and somewhat uncharted innovation in the story; the employees do not seem to know definitively whether their presence will really have an effect on natural history. "Crushing plants could add up infinitesimally. A little error here would multiply in sixty million years, all out of proportion. Of course maybe our theory is wrong. Maybe Time can't be changed by us . . . But until we do know for certain whether our messing around in Time can make a big roar or a little rustle in History, we're being damned careful" (Bradbury 1980, 234–235).

The hunt is successful, but Eckels accidentally strays from the path, getting mud on his shoes. When they return to the present it is apparent that they are in a different reality, that they have altered history. The changes are very subtle at first: there is a chemical smell in the air and the spellings of English words are slightly different. Eckels checks the bottoms of his shoes and sees that he has killed one single butterfly. It is described as "a small thing that could upset balances and knock down a line of small dominoes and then big dominoes and then gigantic dominoes, all down the years across Time." He then learns that the newly elected leader is not Keith (the president when they commenced their journey) but Deutscher, a candidate who was predicted to turn the country into a dictatorship if elected.

In season five the characters who move backward in time initially worry about changing history, but Daniel tells them that "whatever happened, happened" and that they cannot change the course of events, at least not for the current timeline. Unlike Bradbury's "butterfly effect," characters in *Lost* cannot change history by an act of free will. But despite Faraday's explanation, Sayid attempts to change the past by gunning down a young Benjamin Linus. Sayid believes that this will prevent Ben from growing up and influencing the castaways' lives, but true to Daniel's words, fate has its own plan and Ben is saved by the Others. The very act of Sayid shooting Ben likely plays a crucial role in the development of Ben's spiteful nature. Robert Heinlein's novella "By His Bootstraps" illustrates a similar phenomenon by demonstrating the connection between fate and free will in time travel.

"By His Bootstraps"

In this 1941 short story, Bob Wilson is writing his dissertation on time travel when a stranger enters the room through a time portal. Bob is confused at the man's presence but seems to think "Joe" looks familiar. Another man enters through the same entrance and gets into a scuffle with the first, inadvertently knocking Bob through the time portal, to the other side. There, he finds a strange room and a man named Diktor who claims that they are now 30,000 years into the future. Bob falls asleep for a long time in Diktor's chair, and when he wakes up he enters the time portal again, returning to his own room. He sees a man sitting at his desk and realizes that it is himself and that now he is "Joe." He goes through the entire sequence again from the perspective of Joe, discovering he cannot alter the course of events, nor his own actions or words.

This story impels readers to consider their own perception of time. It is typical to visualize time travel in linear terms, but what if we are dealing with a circular image of time, in which the feeling of déjà vu is entirely justified? The feeling that we are repeating, in exact detail, the same actions and words that we have experienced before, maybe multiple times, or from different perspectives is illustrated when the narrator describes returning to his room and realizes that he is re-experiencing the same scene. "This was not simply a similar scene, but the same scene he had lived through once before — save that he was living through it from a different viewpoint" (Heinlein, "By His Bootstraps").

"By His Bootstraps" reflects the unique perception of time as a loop, a concept explored in Friedrich Nietzche's philosophical works.

Nietzsche proposed the idea of the "eternal return" through a hypothetical notion of a demon entering one's room and suggesting the following: "This life as you know it and have lived it, you will have to live once again and innumerable times again; and there will be nothing new in it, but every pain and every joy and every thought and every sigh and everything unspeakably small or great in your life must return to you" (Nietzsche, *The Gay Science* 2001, 194).

In "By His Bootstraps" the main character attempts to defy the past, to change what has already happened but finds it impossible. "Wait a minute now — he was under no compulsion. He was sure of that. Everything he did and said was the result of his own free will. Even if he couldn't remember the script, there were some things he knew 'Joe' hadn't said." But it turns out that he is not capable of changing a single breath or word, a notion that follows Nietzsche's perspective of time. This is an ontological paradox, a temporal loop in which there is no beginning and no end. There is no way to determine which event occurred first because there is no linear timeline on which to base a causal relation. He travels to the future world through the portal again and discovers that there is a time machine that can be manipulated. Upon returning to his room again he finds that he is now the second man he initially met when he was "Bob #1." When he realizes that he has experienced the same scene through three different perspectives, he attempts to continue his paper but is blocked by two perplexing issues: "the problem of the ego and the problem of free will. When there had been three of him in the room, which one was the ego — was himself? And how was it that he had been unable to change the course of events?" In the end, Bob realizes that he is also "Diktor," the man of the distant future, and that he had mentored his younger self so that he would successfully become this man. "His older self had taught his younger self a language which the older self knew because the younger self, after being taught, grew up to be the older self and was, therefore, capable of teaching" (Heinlein, "By His Bootstraps").

The same kind of paradox pervades "All You Zombies," another Heinlein story worth noting in this context. A recurring image in this work is the ouroboros, the snake eating its own tail, a common representation of the loop of time. This symbol can be found in the form of a brooch that *Lost*'s Eloise Hawking wears, an image that foretells the paradox of the Smoke Monster: It was the Smoke Monster in the form of John Locke who told John that he was going "to have to die." Strikingly, the Smoke Monster "found a loophole" in a loop of time, an ontological paradox, a cycle with no beginning and no end. This course of events begins the moment that the Smoke Monster instructs John Locke (via Richard) to leave the island and return after his death ("Because You Left"), but if John Locke had not carried out the task, then the Smoke Monster could never have been there to tell him what to do. In committing suicide John would have fulfilled his fate, not knowing that it was a malevolent prophecy from its inception. Ben pleads with John to not kill himself but changes his mind, succumbing to his long-standing jealousy. John has been told to find Eloise Hawking. And so, it is Ben who carries out the "loophole" plans for the Smoke Monster, murdering John and delivering a suitable body (John Locke's) to the island. The plan works and the Smoke Monster knew it would work, because he set the course of events in motion. Or did he?

Reality check: *A Brief History of Time*

In the season three episode "Not in Portland," one of the Others, a character known as Aldo, is reading Stephen Hawking's *A Brief History of Time*. Although the book is opened to a section on black holes, it can be assumed that this book was chosen to foreshadow the very next episode, "Flashes Before Your Eyes," in which Desmond travels to the past.

In his book, Hawking concludes that it is theoretically possible to travel forward in time: "it is just a matter of engineering: we know it can be done" (Hawking, *A Brief History of Time* 105). Going back in time, however, is a different matter. He doesn't rule out the possibility, but to grossly simplify things, it would be a much more difficult feat to achieve. In any case, Aldo's interest in the text seems to foretell the possibility of the island's capacity to move about in time. It also prefigures the arrival of Daniel Faraday and his mother, Eloise Hawking, both physicists.

Why time travel? Meaning and metaphor

It was only in season five that time traveling became central to *Lost*'s narrative. In prior seasons it was limited to one character's peculiar tendency to become "unstuck" in time. What is the purpose of introducing this device so late in the series? What could it offer audiences besides mind-bending "multiverse" plot twists? To answer this question it is helpful to first explore the suggestive meaning of the journey through space.

Traveling through space (the journey) is an ancient narrative form. The concept of traveling provides structure to any story and it is commonplace to describe narrative as travel, whether the journey is an inward one or an external adventure. This metaphor is so deeply embedded in the reader's consciousness that it is barely notable; all readers expect to follow the narrator down a path of conflict, tension and resolution. A destination is inevitable — eventually the characters arrive somewhere, whether this "place" is abstract (enlightenment, forgiveness, redemption) or tangible (returning home.) In any case, readers understand most stories in terms of movement in space.

But what about the metaphor of time travel? Does the narrative journey through time serve a similar function as the journey through space? Though they both use a term that connotes movement ("travel"), temporal movement carries with it an implication of alteration and the risk of erasure. Instead of the path serving as the sole transformative power, the characters have the capacity to affect the shape and location of the path.

Traveling into the past addresses the human desire to alter history or work through and revisit memories. In Kurt Vonnegut's *Slaughterhouse-Five*, for instance, Billy Pilgrim's rapid movement back and forth in time represents his inability to cope with the devastating memories of World War II. In fact, some critics do not classify this work as science fiction at all. They interpret the science-fiction characteristics of the story — time travel, interaction with alien life forms — as symptoms of schizophrenia or, as Susanne Vees-Gulani suggests, post-traumatic stress disorder. "Being 'spastic in time' thus is a metaphor for Billy's repeatedly re-experiencing the traumatic events he went through in the war, particularly as a POW during the Dresden bombings. Psychologically, Billy has never fully left World War II" (Vees-Gulani 2003).

The first-person narrator of *Slaughterhouse-Five* suggests that time travel represents a need to return to the past and "fix" history, whether on a personal or a global scale. He uses the biblical story of Sodom and Gomorrah as a way to introduce this idea. This book of Genesis story dramatizes an angry god's impending destruction. Before destroying the two cities, God tells Lot to take his family, leave the city and never return. "Lot's wife," the narrator explains, "was told not to look back where all those people and their homes had been. But she *did* look back, and I love her for that, because it was so human" (28). Then he informs the reader that the story he is about to tell, the central narrative of *Slaughterhouse-Five*, was "written by a pillar of salt." Like the unnamed wife of Lot, the narrator, Billy Pilgrim and, perhaps the author too, harbor a need to revisit the past and assess the damage. The purpose of time travel, then, is made explicit in *Slaughterhouse-Five*: to gain perspective and a deeper understanding of what is no longer accessible: the past.

If traveling to the past serves to revisit historical moments and personal memories, then the notion of traveling to the future addresses a preoccupation with prophecy. Another ABC science-fiction program, *Flashforward*, deals unequivocally with predicting the future. It is likely that *Lost*, in fact, borrowed the term "flashforward" from the novel by Rob Sawyer on which the show is based. *Flashforward* is characterized by immediately recognizable religious undertones, specifically reflecting a connection to a biblical passage concerned with prophetic powers. "And it shall come to pass in the last days, saith God, I will pour out of my Spirit upon all flesh: and your sons and your daughters shall prophesy, and your young men shall see visions, and your old men shall dream dreams" (Acts 2.17). This line's striking association with the premise of *Flashforward* illustrates modern science fiction's profound search for meaning through the exploration of time travel.

Of course the notion of prophecy has a long literary tradition, not the least of which is seen in the ancient story of Agamemnon from which the so-called Cassandra effect originates (Aeschylus 1957). Ancient Greek texts, in general, can be credited with many different attributes of *Lost*, in addition to this one. Cassandra is legendary for her foresight and subsequent madness — she can see impending doom but cannot prevent the events from ensuing. Similarly, Desmond Hume in *Lost* is deeply burdened by the dread that comes with his premonitory faculties. After being exposed to a great deal of electromagnetism, he experiences flashes of forthcoming incidents; like Cassandra, he discovers that trying to change the course of events is ultimately futile. *Watership Down* has been referenced more than once in *Lost*, probably for its emphasis on survival and group dynamics, but also because it examines the power of prophecy through its clairvoyant character, Fiver. Fiver's ability to see the future allows a small group to escape the destruction of their warren. He, too, endures a great deal of emotional suffering because of his visions.

The science fiction writer is sometimes considered a modern-day prophet, safely couching his or her predictions in the realm of make-believe. This impression is apparent in *The Time Machine* when the Time Traveller journeys far into the future to a time when the human race is ineffectual and irrelevant in light of extreme technological advancements. He then travels to the end of time as the sun dims and the earth turns to ice. The fascination with prophecy is made explicit in another work by the same author, *The Shape of Things to Come*, a science fiction novel that accurately predicts some of the real-life events of the twentieth century (Wells and Clute 2006). In the novel, a man named Dr. Raven leaves a book of dreams that tell the "history of the future." There is no corporeal time travel in this novel: again, Desmond Hume's experiences come to mind. His ability to travel through space and time by way of consciousness only can be likened to Dr. Raven's dream journeys.

Death by time travel

Some of the characters in *Lost* perish as a result of the unpredictable and intense shifts in time. Why do some die and not others? In Desmond's case it is explained that his "constant," Penny, keeps him alive. Daniel Faraday tells Desmond that "Every equation needs stability, something known. It's called a constant . . . So if you want to stop this, then you need to find something there . . . something that you really, really care about . . . that also exists back here, in 1996" ("The Constant"). George Minkowski, however, does not have someone to stabilize his rapid movement back and forth in time, an ordeal that results in death. Consider, too, Charlotte's vulnerability to the island's movement through space and time. It triggers severe nosebleeds and terrible headaches for her, eventually leading to her death. Do she and Minkowski, and perhaps Daniel Faraday's experimental subject, Teresa, represent those who are unable to confront the past, people who mentally disintegrate under the pressure of history, or, perhaps those who are unable to face dismal projections of the future?

Time travel as a narrative device

As a storytelling mechanism, time travel is not much different from the use of the analepsis (flashback) and the prolepsis (flashforward). It serves much the same purpose, carrying the reader on a non-linear adventure, throwing the audience off balance with extended departures into the past or future. From the beginning of the series, the writers of *Lost* have played with time as an effective narrative device. In the first two seasons, the forward-moving story takes place only on the island, and the memories of each character are dramatized and juxtaposed with the island plot. Thus, the series builds from the middle and works its way out by narrating the story both forward and backward simultaneously. This phenomenon foreshadowed the actual time travel of later seasons; that is, style foretold content, even if this wasn't intentional on the part of the writers.

When "real" time travel was introduced into the series it acted like an enhanced version of the flashback, adding a new layer to the story. Shifting the central narrative to "the past" inverted the idea of the flashback — the time travelers' past actually occurs in the future. The events of the Miles-centric analepsis, for instance, occurs after 1977, so even if the viewers' original point of reference is the year 2004 (or 2007), they are also engaged in a mid-1970s story line, and a period sometime in the early 1980s, off the island. This layering of time periods creates a fuller sense of the whole of the narrative, providing the viewer a more textured understanding of the history from which these characters emerge.

5

"Fathers, Provoke not your Children to Wrath": *Lost* Parents

I don't think there is anything more powerful in film than father–son relationships, maybe even in literature, too.

— *Carlton Cuse*

Daddy, I have had to kill you.

— *Sylvia Plath, "Daddy"*

What better way to enter a conversation about the twisted families portrayed in *Lost* than to recall Sylvia Plath's famous angst-ridden poem with its explicit image of the cruel father as "a ghastly statue"? This classic piece illustrates a roiling-up of bitter emotions toward a presumably harsh father. Though this poem is not referenced in the show, Kate Austen, Penelope Widmore and Sun Kwon would all identify with its speaker, who describes daughterhood thus: "The boot in the face, the brute / Brute heart of a brute like you" and ends with the simple line, "Daddy, daddy, you bastard, I'm through." The enigmatic four-toed statue in *Lost* calls to mind Plath's representation of the father with "one gray toe," a reference to her own father's gangrenous toe. The parent as a "Colossus"[1] reveals something about the island's "father" with its established laws[2] that will be destroyed by the new, emerging generation (i.e. Hurley and Ben). Is the *Lost* statue a representation of the broken, yet oppressive parental figure, an impotent deity that no longer holds sway over the islanders?

In the essay "Dostoevsky and Parricide," Sigmund Freud suggests that "it can scarcely be owing to chance that three of the masterpieces of the literature of all time — the *Oedipus Rex* of Sophocles, Shakespeare's *Hamlet* and Dostoevsky's *The Brothers Karamazov* — should all deal with the same subject: parricide" (107). He asserts that the prevalence of this theme in literary works is due to the universality of the male child's desire to supplant his father in order to secure the attention of his mother. The discussion that follows is certainly not a Freudian criticism of *Lost*; rather, I begin with this particular perspective in order to emphasize the theme of "dysfunctional" parenting as part of a long literary tradition.

Children's stories and myths

The problem of both the father and the mother is found in all media of storytelling, from oral and ancient to digital and interactive. Interesting conflicts find their origin in the deep well of family history, and the rift between parents and children, in particular, is the stuff from which myths and fairy tales are formed. Even in modern-day children's stories, parents don't fare well. Maurice Sendak has said that he fashioned his "wild things" from the impressions adults made on him at a very young age. From young Sendak's perspective adults were huge, unpredictable creatures who inattentively dictated the terms of his existence. In an interview with Bill Moyers, Sendak reveals that he modeled the monsters on his own relatives, who seemed foreign and frightening to him as a child: ". . . these people didn't speak English. And they were unkempt. Their teeth were horrifying . . . hair, unraveling out of their noses. And they'd pick you up and hug you and kiss you, 'Aggghh. Oh, we could eat you up'" (Sendak 2004).

Sendak's point of view emphasizes the distrust and fear with which some children regard parental figures and his stories follow a long tradition of the adults-as-monsters motif in classic fables. This theme is reflected in some of the most well-known protagonists of literature and film, both traditional and popular. Examples of children who are forced to deal with monstrous authority figures include Hansel and Gretel, Little Red Riding Hood and Cinderella. In an interview with Jeff Jensen, *Lost* executive producer, Carlton Cuse reveals this very issue: "I think, mythically speaking, all great heroes have massive daddy issues. Hercules. Oedipus. Luke Skywalker. Indiana Jones. Spider-Man. It all comes with the territory. We dig flawed characters on *Lost*, and a large part of being flawed is the emotional damage inflicted on you by your folks" (Jensen 2007).

Greek mythology abounds with stories of appalling parenthood, fathers and mothers who deceive, abandon and, in some cases, cannibalize their own children. In turn, the children grow up and continue the cycle of violence by destroying and dethroning them, and then terrorizing their own children. The story of abusive families is certainly not a new one. In the famous Athenian tragedy by Sophocles, believed to be first performed around 429 BC (Knox 1956), the parents of Oedipus leave their infant child on a mountain, exposed to the elements, in response to the oracle's prediction that the child would eventually murder his father. But fate (or The Fates) ensures that this prophecy is fulfilled, and when Oedipus reaches adulthood, after being adopted and raised by another family, unknowingly faces his father and then murders him, thinking he is an enemy.

The patricide motif is found in many stories about not only men, but gods too — they are fated to defeat or destroy their fathers. Cronus, for instance, castrated his father, Uranus, and overthrew him, making himself king of the Titans. In turn, Cronus's son, Zeus, "dethroned him and seized power for himself" banishing the father to the underworld. And anyone familiar with Greek mythology cannot forget what a monstrous father Cronus turned out to be. In order to make sure that his own children would not threaten his power, Cronus ate each of them upon their births, until his wife, Rhea, tricked him into eating a rock instead of baby Zeus (Hamilton 1969).

The Dead Father

In an episode recap during season three, Jeff Jensen suggests Donald Barthelme's postmodern work *The Dead Father* as a fitting novel to illustrate how fatherhood is presented in *Lost* ("the book that has *Lost* written all over it"): "The dead father in *The Dead Father* is symbolic of so many things that shape and form us — bad parents, corrupt institutions, f — -ed up philosophies. I believe *Lost* shares those same thematic concerns" (Jensen 2007). The novel, a work of experimental fiction published in the 1960s, actually has an old fashioned plot structure and characters. To be sure, it is a strange idea for a cast of characters to be charged with chaperoning a huge statue-like man, 3,200 cubits or 1.4 kilometers, named the "dead father" (though he is very much alive — "dead, but still with us, still with us, but dead" (3) on a long journey to a giant gravesite where he is going to be buried. This looming figure is very father-like indeed, in the particular sense, but he also represents the idea of a collective father, including both political and spiritual authority. The story can be interpreted as the overthrowing of a tyrannical leader, the death of a god, or the death of a repressive institution and the emergence of a new way of life. Indeed, *The Dead Father* is simply a circle-of-life story, a sloughing off of the old skin to reveal a new generation (Barthelme 1975).

Within this novel there is a fictitious "Manual for Sons" that provides a number of profoundly comical "tips" for sons to follow in order for them to achieve this end: "You must become your father, but a paler, weaker version of him" (146). The manual insists that adult sons are generally angry at their fathers, so angry in fact that the potential for patricide is ever-present. Here, the narrator ponders the reasons for the son's madness. "He is mad about being small when you were big, but no, that's not it, he is mad about being helpless when you were not helpless, but no, not that either, he is mad about being contingent when you were necessary, not quite it, he is insane because when he loved you, you didn't notice" (143).

This last line, situated in an otherwise bizarre and deeply satirical work, is straightforward and truthful. A child's unacknowledged and unrequited love for a parent has the potential to grow into a monstrous, parricidal presence in the adult child's psyche, as we see with Benjamin Linus in *Lost*. This also recalls the relationship with his spiritual father, Jacob. Ben feels that he has been exceedingly faithful and obedient to Jacob, doing everything he asks. Shortly before killing Jacob, he demands, in a very child-like way, "What was so wrong with me? What about me?" — to which Jacob replies "What *about* you?" ("The Incident"). This final statement is more than Ben can bear — presumably he interprets these words to mean that Jacob believes him to be irrelevant and inconsequential. Ben's fragile ego is unable to withstand such an insult from a man that he worshiped and obeyed for so long, but who was so powerful in contrast with Ben's weaknesses. He must kill Jacob to be free of the wound inflicted upon him.

The daughters in *Lost* should not be ignored when it comes to this particular brand of madness. Certainly Sun and Penny seem to harbor the same bitter feelings toward their fathers that Ben and John do, and Kate actually acts upon those feelings. But in *The Dead Father*, one particular line clearly illustrates the issues that all of the characters have faced: "Fathers are like blocks of marble, giant cubes, highly polished, with veins and seams, placed squarely in your path. They block your path. They cannot be climbed over neither can they be slithered past. They are the past" (129). Without doubt, Daniel Faraday is unable to sidestep Eloise or Charles. Sun always finds resistance when it comes to her father. Jack cannot escape his father's shadow or his father's words even long after Christian's death.

Corrupt parents: targets of parricide

The young hero who unearths a shadowy and dangerous side of his family history is a common motif in both ancient mythology and popular culture, generally recognized as an inevitable coming-to-terms with the past. Luke Skywalker, for example, finds out that his own father was drawn to the dark side, tempted by the allure of power. In *The Brothers Karamazov*, Alyosha, the youngest legitimate son of Fyodor Karamazov must acknowledge the fact that, despite his own dedication to God and the monastery, he is still a Karamazov, a name that the townspeople, at least, associate with immorality and debauchery. In Aldous Huxley's *Island*, the good doctor of the community recalls his wretched pre-island life in which his father engaged in brutal acts of repression in the name of a "civilized" way of life.

When the characters of *Lost* discover sinister tendencies in their parents they attempt to destroy either the guilty parent or the deviant inclination. The detection of moral deficiency in a parent, or ongoing repression in a family setting, furnishes the story with a good deal of plausible character motive. Kate Austen and Benjamin Linus both commit premeditated patricide; John Locke murders his father indirectly, yet intentionally; the Man in Black stabs to death his adoptive mother; and several other characters attempt to defeat and sometimes supplant their fathers (Sun, Jack, Penny).

Kate perpetrates a similar act to that of Oedipus, though hers is more calculated. She perceives her stepfather to be an intruder, an outsider and an enemy to herself and her mother. To be sure, Wayne is an abusive man and Diane's life is probably in danger, but what Kate does not realize when she kills him is that Wayne is, in truth, her biological father.

In a way, Ben Linus commits parricide twice — he kills his real father, Roger, and then he kills his leader and mentor, Jacob, the father of the island. It is not necessary to consult Freud for an interpretation: it is clear that Ben would supplant Jacob if given the chance. The same man is also partially responsible for a third parricide being committed. In "The Brig" he challenges John to kill his own father as a rite of initiation into the Others' group. He encourages John to commit murder by reminding him of all the transgressions that Cooper has committed against John.[3] This prefigures the scene in "The Incident, Part 1," when John (as the Smoke Monster) persuades Ben to kill Jacob, pointing out all of the failures of Jacob, the man who has served as a father figure for Ben through all of his years leading the Others. In reply to Ben's uncertainty about killing Jacob, John makes a case for why Ben should commit the murder: "Because, despite your loyal service to this island, you got cancer. You had to watch your own daughter gunned down right in front of you. And your reward for those sacrifices? You were banished . . . So the question is, Ben, why the hell *wouldn't* you want to kill Jacob?" ("The Incident, Part 1"). In the season three episode "The Brig," the roles are reversed, with Ben trying to convince John that he needed to kill his father, Anthony Cooper.

> Ben: John. The hesitation that you're feeling is just the part of you that still feels like he had a perfectly good explanation for stealing your kidney. Throwing you out of an eight-story window. Don't you wanna be free from him?
>
> John: Why are you doing this to me?
>
> Ben: You're doing this to yourself. As long as he's still breathing, you'll still be that same sad pathetic little man that was kicked off his Walkabout tour because you couldn't walk.

This motif, parricide to achieve liberation, John killing his father "to be free of him," is not necessarily an original source of narrative conflict. If the subsequent scene — John Locke entering the camp carrying the corpse of his father on his back — seems bizarre to the average television viewer, we can recognize here that it evokes the dead fathers of *Lost*'s narrative forebears.

The Brothers Karamazov

Significantly, John, Jack and Ben are the characters present when the first allusion to the great Fyodor Dostoevsky arises. Each of these men has his counterpart in the novel that John offers Ben (*The Brothers Karamazov*), and all of them have suffered at the hands of a harsh father, a conflict central to this epic work by Dostoevsky. In this season two episode, Ben is being held hostage by the castaways in a vault at the Swan station ("Maternity Leave"). When John and Jack enter the vault to check on him, John tosses a copy of *The Brothers Karamazov* on Ben's cot. There is a brief literary moment here, drawing the audience's attention to Dostoevsky's final novel, considered by most critics to be his best work. Ben says, with a bit of a huff, "Dostoevsky. Got any Stephen King?"

Locke: Just something to pass the time. Did you know that
         Hemingway was jealous of Dostoevsky?
Jack: No, John, I didn't know that.
Locke: He wanted to be the world's greatest writer, but
         convinced himself that he could never get out from
         under Dostoevsky's shadow.

Though this dialogue does not address the novel's content, the presence of such a work within a text that deals considerably with parent–child conflicts instructs the audience to draw thematic comparisons between the novel and the series. This self-reflexive practice contextualizes the narrative of *Lost* within a literary history by engaging the audience's awareness of a significant work.

The Brothers Karamazov is an epic tale about family, fatherhood, patricide and the value of community. It addresses the question of our responsibility to others and draws attention to human weakness and the inherent tendency to inflict grief and pain on one another, knowingly and willingly. The themes this novel has in common with *Lost* are countless — free will, redemption and sacrifice to name a few — but I will focus on the more secular theme of parenthood and human relationships in general. *The Brothers Karamazov* addresses a societal ill that troubled Dostoevsky: bad parenting. Though considered common knowledge in the realm of modern-day child psychology, Dostoevsky knew that parents draw the blueprints for their children's lives, setting a wheel in motion that will end in suffering or joy, or, as is usually the case, a little of both. Parents are the original source of all faults and strengths, and their actions have ramifications that ripple beyond the nuclear family and across succeeding generations. In a letter to an anonymous mother Dostoyevsky expressed his concerns about the disintegration of the "modern family" (Terras 2002, 60). He makes the claim that if a child comes to his mother at age 16 asking why he should love her, she has already failed as a parent. Every mystery about every individual can be traced back to the childhood environment and the genetic history of a family. Like John carrying the dead weight of his father on his back, all individuals must carry the weight of their family skeletons.

In "What Do Jack and Locke Owe Their Fathers?" an essay published in *Lost and Philosophy*, Michael Austin concludes that both Jack and Locke were deprived of the love and nurturing that a father should provide. "Their fathers, in fact, failed to fulfill their parental obligations to their sons" (Austin 2008, 17). Clearly this is the case for

John Locke whose father left him to be raised in foster care, conned
him out of a kidney when he was an adult, and then pushed John out
of a window, paralyzing him. If any one of the father characters on
Lost could be compared to Dostoevsky's patriarch, Fyodor Karamazov,
"one of the most loathsome characters in all literature," it is Anthony
Cooper, the con artist and father of John Locke (Dostoevsky, *The
Brothers Karamazov* 1999, back cover).

Fyodor Karamazov is the father of three legitimate sons and possibly one illegitimate son who works for him as a servant. He is a terrible
husband and a completely absent father. From abuse and neglect he
drives away his first wife, leaving him with their three-year-old son,
Dmitri, whom he promptly deserts. The unnamed narrator, serving as
a collective voice for the townspeople, tells the reader, "He completely
abandoned the child of his marriage with Adelaide, not from spite,
nor because of his matrimonial grievances, but because he simply
forgot about him" (Dostoevsky, *The Brothers Karamazov* 1999, 22).
Like John Locke, Dmitri grows up in several different homes and it is
not until he "comes of age" that he meets his father for the first time.
Dmitri believes he has been cheated out of his inheritance in the same
way that Locke feels cheated and abandoned by Anthony Cooper. Old
Karamazov has two more legitimate sons by another wife but when she
dies he abandons them too. There is debate surrounding the paternity
of the fourth son, Smerdyakov, but Old Karamazov does not object to
the accusations that he is the father. Smerdyakov, whose mother ("the
village idiot") dies in childbirth, is adopted and raised by the servants
of Karamazov.

Among other things, this novel is a murder mystery interested
more in exploring the motives of the possible murderers than in identifying the perpetrator. Ultimately, it is Dmitri who stands charged
with the act of patricide. Although there is plenty of evidence to support a motive in Dmitri's case, it is revealed later that it was actually
Smerdyakov who killed the father. Like Sawyer and Ben, Smerdyakov
has a lifetime of grievances that motivate the murder of this man. But
more important than identifying a single guilty party is acknowledging
the collective responsibility of all involved. Through the story of these
brothers and their community, Dostoevsky demonstrates the notion
that "all are responsible for all" and that it was not just one man who
had a hand in the murder, but the whole community who contributed
to the problem. "Everyone is really responsible to all men and for all
men for everything." Ivan, the intellectual, realizes that he, too, played
a role in the murder of his father by provoking Smerdyakov's hatred for

Fyodor. On a subconscious level, Ivan understands that Smerdyakov is poised to commit the murder, but he does nothing to stop it.

The season three episode "The Brig" conveys a similar moral, revealing that several men are responsible for the death of Anthony Cooper. With its "magic box" and Ben's decree that John carry his dead father on his back, this particular episode is somewhat peculiar. It is fantastic and archetypal, John carrying the full weight of a dead Anthony Cooper on his back, in contrast with the more realistic tone of the first couple of seasons. Looking at it through the lens of Dostoevsky's work, viewers can see the same message that the defendant conveys in Dmitri's trial. Everyone involved has a hand in the murder of Anthony Cooper — Ben and his henchmen kidnap Cooper and bring him to the island, Ben orders John to kill his father, Richard encourages him to do the same and John convinces Sawyer to carry out the act. But Anthony Cooper himself is also responsible; he bears some of the guilt for Sawyer's life of desperate crime and for John's long-time suffering. He has caused irreversible emotional damage in the lives of both of these men, but even when facing death, Cooper denies his guilt.

In *The Brothers Karamazov* Dmitri's defending attorney, Fetyskovisch, points out that it was partly the father's fault for neglecting his children so severely. He provides a quote from the book of Ephesians, a cautionary passage warning, "Fathers, provoke not your children to wrath." The attorney continues the defense by explaining,

> Yes, let us first fulfill Christ's injunction ourselves and only then venture to expect it of our children. Otherwise we are not fathers, but enemies of our children, and they are not our children, but our enemies, and we have made them our enemies ourselves. . . . let us say plainly, the father is not merely he who begets the child, but he who begets it and does his duty by it. (702)

Consider the hypothetical question posed by Fetyskovisch about fathers: "Why am I bound to love him, simply for begetting me when he has cared nothing for me all my life?" (703). In *Lost* many characters might ask themselves this question, including Sun, Kate, Penny, Ben and Daniel. The defense attorney also asserts that poor fathering is linked to the various social ills of the community. Many of the "*Lost* parents" seem heartless and detached, but worse, some of these fathers and mothers are responsible for tragedies of far-reaching and massive proportions. Penny's father, Charles, rejects Desmond and forces the two lovers apart. As a result, Desmond despairingly sets out for a journey around the world but lands on the island, setting into motion a catastrophic series of events. Christian Shephard continually discourages his son Jack and tells him that he "just doesn't have what it takes." The long-term effect is that Jack grows into an obsessive, controlling and unhappy adult, making other people miserable in turn. Sun's repressive father ruins her marriage by way of his strict standards and corrupt profession and, consequently, Sun attempts to escape her father's control by leaving the country and her husband. In the course of events, she has an affair with another man, further devastating the marriage. But the parent whose act has the most monumental effect is the unnamed adoptive mother of Jacob and the Man in Black. She is, in part, responsible for the making of the Smoke Monster, an entity described as "evil incarnate" ("Sundown" Dogen) who haunts the island for more than a thousand years.

Spiritual fathers

In *The Brothers Karamazov* Father Zosima plays a central role in Alyosha Karamazov's life. He serves to fill the gap left by Alyosha's biological father, Fyodor, and shares a number of valuable lessons with Alyosha, transferring wisdom from one generation to the next. He can be compared to *Lost*'s Jacob, who functions as mentor and guide, a spiritual and intellectual father of Richard, Ilana, the Others, and the castaway candidates, particularly Hurley. Ilana tells Ben that Jacob was the closest thing to a father that she ever had ("Dr. Linus"). But Ben also depended on Jacob as the all-knowing, all-powerful god and father of the island. In contrast to Jacob, the Smoke Monster is a devious father figure, who destroys and leads astray the "children" of the island. He wants to kill "the good father" but must persuade one of the islanders to do it for him. As mentioned earlier, Ben's act of murdering Jacob is akin to patricide. Ben can be likened to Smerdyakov Karamazov, because he, too, feels cheated out of his inheritance; he is not chosen as a candidate, nor has he been acknowledged by Jacob for all he has done for the island.

An adoptive family: the Charlie trinity

Desmond's familial background is unknown; there is no flashback that tells viewers about his parents or childhood. Further, he does not seem to identify with a grouping of characters or seem to belong in one clan or another. The castaways accept him as one of them, though he is decidedly separate. Charles Widmore acts as an ever-present parental figure for Desmond, a force, however unpleasant, that influences Desmond's development. Desmond's love for Penny ordains his connection to Charles, for better or worse. All of these people, on and off the island, become Desmond's adoptive family, but I will focus on only three of them in the following passage.

Although we have seen duplicate names throughout the series, no repeated names are as significant as the three Charlies. The presence of this trinity seems to have a bearing on the shape of Desmond's life, whether in one universe or another. The most famous trinity known to modern Western civilization is, of course, the Holy Trinity, but the term can apply to any three-fold entity or triad of significance. This particular grouping of three, in respect to Desmond, can be compared to the sacred version: Charles Widmore is the father, Charlie Hume is the son and Charlie Pace is the Holy Spirit. Charles is very much like an Old Testament god and father — committing questionable acts of violence and aggression for the "greater good," especially towards Desmond. Charlie Hume represents the child as savior (of Desmond) and the hope of a good father–son relationship. Charlie Pace acts as a guiding spirit, relaying important messages to Desmond but always remaining a mystery. In the original timeline Charlie saves Desmond and connects him to Penny, as bearer of her message. In the afterlife Charlie saves him by showing him "the truth" and, again, steers him toward Penny. This metaphysical family is a web that, like any family, at once supports Desmond and frustrates him.

The Turn of the Screw

This nineteenth-century psychological thriller/ghost tale by Henry James takes place at an isolated country estate where two orphaned children live with their ineffectual, mentally unstable governess. If this does not sound comparable to our castaway story, consider this: in a sense, all of the survivors are abandoned on the island, left for dead by the rest of the world to fend against the insane guardians of the island. Figuratively, many of them were like orphaned children to begin with, even before the crash of flight 815.[4] Consider, too, that in *The Turn of the Screw* there is an indistinct haunting of the estate, though the reader is never sure what Henry James had in mind: are there really ghosts or is the narrator, the unnamed governess, simply crazy? Is this a ghost story or a case of child abuse? This is a topic that will be addressed in more detail in the following chapter, but it is relevant here in terms of incompetent parenting. Depending on one's interpretation of the story, either the governess is incapable of defending the children against the malevolent apparitions, or she is simply insane — in the latter case, not only is she unfit to protect the children, she is a danger to them and thus becomes the monster of the tale, much like the adoptive mother of Jacob and his brother, a woman driven mad from isolation and the burden of guarding the island.

6

"We're All Mad Here": Dreams, Illusions and the Nature of Reality

Let's consider who it was that dreamed it all . . . it must have been either me or the Red King. He was part of my dream of course — but then I was part of his dream too!
— Through the Looking-Glass and
What Alice Found There

In the last chapter of C. S. Lewis's *The Great Divorce*, the reader discovers that the narrator's long journey through the afterlife was no more than a dream. The unnamed protagonist has spent the length of the narrative trying to unearth the true nature of existence, only to realize that the entire experience was merely an illusion. "A dream? Then — then — am I not really here, Sir?" he asks the spirit guide.[1] The spirit affirms his suspicion but notes that they did, indeed, get a glimpse of the truth: "Ye saw the choices a bit more clearly than ye could see them on earth: the lens was clearer. But it was still seen through the lens. Do not ask of a vision in a dream more than a vision in a dream can give" (Lewis 1945, 116). Here, the spirit is conveying a twofold message. First, he acknowledges that this dream is a clearer lens for perceiving truth than the lens of waking life, which suggests the second notion: that the material world is an illusion, no less "real" than imaginative visions and nighttime dreams. This chapter explores how dreams and illusions reveal "truth" in fictional texts and how the dream narrative operates in *Lost*.

The dream as a narrative device

The series is infused with themes and images from *Alice's Adventures in Wonderland*, *Through the Looking-Glass and What Alice Found There* and the film adaptation of Frank L. Baum's *The Wonderful Wizard of*

Oz, all dream narratives. Their placement and citation in *Lost* urges the viewer to consider the significance of the show's presentation of dreams and illusions. The supernatural phenomena in these children's stories are explained as the workings of a sleeping mind.[2] Attributing an entire story to an individual's dream is sometimes convenient narrative tool, but for the modern viewer or reader this device might seem unoriginal and simplistic, providing a crude explanation for the fantastic elements of a story. Nonetheless, symbolic expressions of the internal human experience provide the story with a raw sense of mystery and the sublime, without slipping into the genre of horror. These include not only dreams, but also visions, hallucinations and prophecy, phenomena usually construed as signs of mental illness or drug use in real life. But in fiction, meaning *can* be derived from madness and the elements of the dream serve to create richly textured moods and an expanded understanding of characters and themes.

Dreams in *Lost*

Although viewers would be disappointed to see the entire series explained away as one long nightmare, the brief dream sequences within single episodes provide uncanny glimpses into the heart of *Lost*, using archetypal images to capture the audience's attention. Some elements of the story are revealed more effectively in psychological terms; these are ideas that are conveyed more readily through symbols, images and sound in the bizarre setting of a dream, where the laws of science, logic and morality need not apply. In his essay "The Symbolic Language of Dreams" Stephen King says, "I've always used dreams the way you'd use mirrors to look at something you couldn't see head on" (King 2004, 18).

In the early episodes of *Lost*, nightmares provide emotional weight to the mysteries of the island, particularizing the sublime by depicting it through one character's perspective. In "Deus Ex Machina" John Locke's dream prophesies Boone's tragedy and reveals clues about the downed plane with heroin-filled Virgin Mary statuettes on board. In the dream, Boone is shown with a bloodied face; he is repeating the haunting phrase, "Theresa falls up the stairs, Theresa falls down the stairs." The camera cuts to a woman in a full-length coat standing in the jungle. At this angle, the viewer is watching the disturbing images through Locke's eyes, experiencing the scene as the dreamer. The woman's hand moves in an unnatural, rapid motion as she points skyward. This peculiar computer-generated effect makes for the most sinister image of the dream sequence. In film, irregular movement, especially sudden jerking motions portray the subject as grotesque and sometimes dangerous. Suddenly, in the dream, John is in his wheelchair and discovers that he can't move his legs. With an expression of terror in his eyes, he struggles to escape and then begins to fall. The viewer can identify closely with John at this point, given that both paralysis and the impression of falling are common sensations of the human dream. This waking moment marks a return to the more realistic world of the island but leaves the viewer on edge, with the sense of danger that accompanies a particularly vivid nightmare, even after the dreamer acknowledges it as fantasy.

The nightmare extends into John's waking life, revealing a truth about both the past and the future. First, the image of Boone's face smeared with blood foretells his death. Second, John learns that his dream reflects something that only Boone would know — Boone feels responsible for a terrible injury and possible death that happened years ago, involving a woman named Theresa. In the dream, John also sees an incoming plane, presumably Yemi's drug-running plane, just before it crashed. This dream, then, is at once a vision of the island's history and a prophecy of the near future. It depicts the mystical powers of the island and creates a sense that something menacing is looming over these characters.

Otherworldly or other worlds?

In light of later complications to the plot, a different mode of interpreting John's visions becomes plausible. Bearing in mind the elements of time travel and alternate realities, it is possible that this dream is not just a vague prediction, but a clear window to a different time or dimension. John's dreams seem to be prophetic in the simpler context of the early seasons, but later, the audience discovers that much of what he sees has already happened (or is always happening[3]). For instance, the dream in which John finds Horace building a cabin in the middle of the jungle plays like a loop, as if Horace is doomed to repeat the same actions and lines for eternity. He turns around, blood dripping from his nose, and tells John that he (Horace) has been dead for 12 years. After seeing the time-traveling episodes of season five, viewers might conclude that Horace was not an image in a dream, but rather a hiccup in time, or a spirit condemned to the same spot forever. And taking into account season six, one can interpret this dream as a manipulation of the Smoke Monster. In the dream Horace says, "You gotta find me, John. You gotta find me. And when you do, you'll find him [Jacob]" ("Cabin Fever").

If the dream then serves as a portal to another universe, a complete reality on its own terms, how does one determine which one is "more real"? This is a question that explicitly presents itself in season six when there is undeniably more than one reality. Is it possible that dreams are windows to these parallel or metaphysical worlds? The episodes of déjà vu, which many of the "flash sideways" characters seem to experience when they examine their reflections in the glass, also serve as a vision of another existence. This "looking-glass" experience explained as an entirely *Other* world is emphasized by Lewis Carroll's work being prominently featured again in the last season ("Lighthouse").

The island: whose dream is it anyway?

In *Through the Looking-Glass and What Alice Found There* Tweedledee and Tweedledum tell Alice that she exists only in the Red King's dream and that if he woke up she would "go out — bang — just like a candle!" (Carroll 2002, 162). "You're only one of the things in his dream. You know very well you're not real," says Tweedledum (163). Alice ultimately rejects this notion, but it provides a provocative interpretation of the narrative. Who is dreaming whom? Who or what creates the dreams of prophetic vision and deep insight? Applying this interpretation to *Lost*, viewers might wonder if the entire narrative is one character's dream. The writers hinted at this notion in "Dave," an episode that played with the possibility of the story as the hallucination of a madman, suggesting that Hurley imagined the whole story from his room in the Santa Rosa Mental Hospital. Some fans have suggested that the series is the dream of Vincent the dog, an interesting idea considering Vincent's perspective and his presence from the first moment of the pilot episode to one of the last images in the finale episode. But we could also explore the notion that the island is doing the dreaming. Perhaps it is using the characters as vessels to receive certain messages. In this case, John's dreams are not his at all; rather, they are generated by the island and he is merely a dream catcher. Consider Claire's dream, when John tells her that if she gives up her baby for adoption, "everyone pays the price" ("Raised by Another") or Charlie's dream that compels him to save baby Aaron ("Fire + Water"). These visions seem to be conjured up by the island in order to protect the child, recalling Lewis Carroll's personification of animals and inanimate objects. The island as a character, a dreaming character no less, is indeed reminiscent of Wonderland.

What function do dreams serve in stories? In real life, they seem to be arbitrary collections of images and words and superficial reflections of the waking life. But Jungian theory supports the idea that dreams are important representations of our desires, fears, anxieties and passion. The archetypes — exaggerated recurring images, characters or places — reveal ideas that can only be conveyed in symbols (Jung 1990). In fictional narratives, dreams convey a good deal about character, setting or theme in a relatively short passage or abbreviated time frame. For instance, in Claire's dream, ("Raised by Another"), the audience learns that Claire and her child are in danger, that there are larger implications in her decision to give up the baby for adoption and that there is a battle between good and evil, as symbolized by the black and white eyes of John Locke. Even if this information is not considered factual within the story, the possibility of these ideas has been introduced to the viewer.

Wonderland and Oz: identity and imagination

In Lewis Carroll's *Through the Looking-Glass and What Alice Found There*, the people from Alice's real life are manifested as kings, queens and talking animals. She works out her interior conflicts and coming-of-age struggles within a fantasy world in the same way that the characters of *Lost* bring their personal struggles with them through time, space and even to the afterlife. The looking glass or mirror serves as Alice's portal to another world, a place where she can work through the fundamental issues of a growing child, addressing the basic questions about how the grown-up world operates. How should she interpret the language of adults? How will she assert her influence on the world? The land beyond the looking glass comes across as absurd to the reader, but the adult world can be just as befuddling to a child. On the other side of the glass, Alice finds an inverted reflection of everything in her own world. It is spring on one side, winter on the other. Her side is tidy and the other unkempt. Most significant, objects that are normally inanimate have come to life and Alice is able to interact with everything that speaks. In non-looking-glass society she is constrained by manners and adult protocol, not allowed to speak until she is first addressed by an adult.

In the same way, the characters of *Lost* are allowed more freedom to self-actualize on the island. Even if the island is not meant to be interpreted as a dream or a fantasy world, the place is obviously enchanted and otherworldly compared to the characters' pre-crash lives. It is dreamlike to viewers and characters alike, and serves the same metaphorical purpose as Alice's looking-glass world. The characters are able to work out their issues on a mythological scale and their problems seem more readily solvable. For instance, to address immediate concerns like the need for food, drink and security, John hunts, Jack finds water and a natural shelter, and Jin catches fish. All of the characters have the capacity to build fires, to cook and to protect one another. These are activities they never had to think about in their pre-island lives, but they all find a sense of fulfillment as they practice basic survival skills and contribute in a meaningful way to this new community. In short, their lives take on greater significance when they are faced with the simple task of keeping each other alive.

Alice, too, finds a sense of meaning in her looking-glass life. She takes charge and solves problems without relying on authority figures. She deals with petulant characters and absurd puzzles, but finds her way, ultimately becoming Queen and standing up to the Red Queen, who is transformed into a harmless kitten as Alice awakens. She returns to her reality with a new sense of authority over her own life, even though the reader presumes that Alice was playing with the kittens and chess pieces all along, and that the looking-glass world exists only in her imagination.

Likewise, in the final passages of *Alice's Adventures in Wonderland*, the predecessor to *Through the Looking-Glass*, the reader learns that the story was only a dream. The narrator then turns the point of view around and addresses the audience directly. "'Oh, I've had such a curious dream!' said Alice, and she told her sister, as well as she could, all these strange Adventures of hers that you have just been reading about" (Carroll 2002, 107). The passages that follow this quote chronicle the unnamed sister's attempt to dream Alice's dream. But the sister only "half believed herself in Wonderland." Her eyes are closed as she dreams, but unlike Alice, "she knew she had but to open them again, and all would change to dull reality" (109). Alice's sister denies the dream, robbing it of its potency.

Similarly, Jack Shephard's inability to see the island as a significant entity with transcendent powers compels the audience to question the value of the story. Should they believe in the dream world, an outlandishly furnished metaphysical island? What would compel any of these characters to return to the island? As Jack asks John in season two's "Orientation," "Why do you find it so easy [to believe]?" Later on, in "Dr. Linus" when Jack urges Richard Alpert to light the dynamite, Jack seems to be testing the nature of the island, to see if his experience is just an illusion. In essence, he is challenging the reality of the island and the significance of the dream, urging the viewer to do the same.

Like Alice's story, Dorothy's dream in the *The Wizard of Oz*, is a direct reflection of her real life. This notion is made explicit in the film, if not in Baum's original story. All of the farm characters have their counterparts in the land of Oz and are played by the same actors. Though the mirror is not used as a symbol in *The Wizard of Oz*, the film illustrates two worlds that directly reflect one another (Judy Garland, *The Wizard of Oz* [home video] 1999).

The Wizard of Oz makes clear what is not necessarily explicit in the Alice stories — that the young girl is trying to understand and navigate the adult world through the fantasy of an alternate world. All of the adults in Dorothy's life have corresponding characters in the Land of Oz. The farmhands are illustrated as Dorothy's three travelling companions, the Tin Man, the Cowardly Lion and the Scarecrow. The Gales' unfriendly neighbor, Almira Gulch, is represented by the Wicked Witch of the West. And, of course, the traveling Professor Marvel is reflected as the false wizard and political leader of Oz. The dream as a reflection provides the viewer with insight into Dorothy's "real" existence, her life on the farm.

Similarly, in season six of *Lost* there are two worlds — one that appears to be symbolic and mythical, and one that is more realistic. The dichotomy has changed from pre-crash life versus island life to island life versus afterlife. This newer reality, what has been deemed a "flash sideways" world, is not a dream, nor is it to be construed as a figment of imagination. In the realm of this narrative, it is supposedly an in-between place, a sort of limbo between life and an existence that lies far beyond the physical world. The emerging symbol of the mirror in season six indicates that these worlds reflect one another, even if the looking glass is sometimes warped. On one side of the mirror Ethan Goodspeed is a well-intentioned obstetrician; on the other he is a spy, kidnapper and murderer. Likewise, Benjamin Linus is a frustrated, yet good-hearted high school teacher on one side, but a psychopathic despot on the other. John has faith, John lacks faith; Jack is patient, Jack is impatient; Alex's life is destroyed, Alex's life is saved; Hurley is lucky, Hurley is unlucky; and so on. As in Alice's looking glass, everything is strikingly familiar but it all "goes the wrong way" (Carroll 2002, 123). Or, more accurately, it all goes "the right way" in this new reality; for the most part, all of the characters seem happier and more at peace, evidently because they have been working through their issues for some time, beyond the grave.

Hallucinations and voices: "An Occurrence at Owl Creek Bridge"

He distinctly heard whispers.
    — "An Occurrence at Owl Creek Bridge" (Bierce 1970, 52)

The most significant aspect of Ambrose Bierce's short work of fiction, "An Occurrence at Owl Creek Bridge,"[4] is its psychological tension, but it is the timing of the narrative that helps to produce the astonishing ending. The entire sequence of hallucinations takes place in the time it takes to kill a man by hanging. The central character, Peyton Farquhar, a Confederate soldier from whose perspective the story is told, is standing on Owl Creek Bridge with a rope around his neck, waiting for his execution. When he falls, the rope breaks and he escapes. He swims down the river and runs all night until he reaches his home, where his wife waits for him on the front porch. During this long, strange journey the man describes a great pain in his neck that reaches down through his extremities. Towards the end, though, he feels that the road is soft, almost as if he is treading on air. It turns out he is doing just that; as he moves to embrace his wife, the pain in his neck returns and "a blinding white light blazes all about him with a sound like the shock of a cannon — then all is darkness and silence" (Bierce 1970, 53). The man is dead with a broken neck, swinging from Owl Creek Bridge.

Though the ending is a shock, when readers return to the previous passages, they find a good bit of evidence that the entire journey is hallucinatory in nature. The narrator provides a clear description of the familiar, yet unfamiliar, settings we find in dreams: "He had not known that he lived in so wild a region. There was something uncanny in the revelation" (52). In his vision, everything is described as symmetrical. Along the road, the trees are positioned in exceptionally straight lines and in the "garden plants" on the bank of the river "he noted a definite arrangement." The trees form a direct line to the horizon

> . . . like a diagram in a lesson in perspective. Overhead, as he looked up through this rift in the wood, shone great golden stars looking unfamiliar and grouped in strange constellations. He was sure they were arranged in some order which had a secret and malign significance. The wood on either side was full of

singular noises, among which — once, twice, and again — he
distinctly heard whispers in an unknown tongue. (52)

This last line especially conjures up images of the island as an illu-
sory state of mind. There are so many improbable events, so many
coincidences, that it seems it could not be anything but a hallucinatory vision. The fact that this book is tucked into the series between
"Fire + Water," a Charlie-centric episode brimming with dreams and
hallucinations and "Dave," an episode based on Hurley's imaginary
friend, situates it as a clue that sheds some light on the writers' intentions, and even presages the end ("The End") when Christian provides
the revelation, both to Jack and the viewer, that they are dead. The
moment Jack remembers his last few breaths of life are as surprising
and heartbreaking as Peyton Farquhar's flash of realization that yanks
his consciousness back to the instant of his death.

Apparitions: a sampling of famous literary ghosts

The stories offered thus far are distinctly and definitively dreams-as-
narratives. The following pages will approach the ghosts of *Lost* not as
visions or hallucinations conjured up by the mind, but as supernatural
apparitions — real, live spirits in the tradition of old-fashioned ghost
stories. I will examine the history of ghosts in literature through
three different narratives — *The Odyssey*, *Hamlet* and *The Turn of the
Screw*.

Homer's *Odyssey* is one of the earliest recorded narratives of Western
literature. The ghostly part of this epic poem is Odysseus' voyage to
the underworld where he meets several apparitions, including his own
mother's spirit. The description of this afterlife and the meeting point
between life and death is more gloomy and depressing than it is fear-
some. Unlike the hell of many modern-day religions, this dwelling is
not so much to be feared as accepted as an inevitable destination for
the soul. Twice Odysseus refers to the spirits as "poor feckless ghosts"
and the ghost of Tiresius asks Odysseus, "Why have you left the light
of day and come down to visit the dead in this sad place?" (Homer,
The Odyssey 1944, 132–133) Still, Odysseus is affected by the eerie
strangeness of it all: "[the ghosts] came from every quarter and flitted
about with a strange kind of screaming that made me turn pale with
fear" (132).

Odysseus sits and speaks to his mother's spirit as she tells him all
that has come to pass since he left home. She warns him of the dangers

that await him at home and advises him to be cautious upon his return. Tiresius foretells of a perilous passage home and provides Odysseus with very specific prophecies about each dilemma he will face. Thus, two things can be concluded about these early literary ghosts: one, that readers and listeners of this story likely believed in a spiritual life beyond the material world and, two, that these spirits hold powers of omniscience with unlimited visions of time and space.

Roughly two thousand years later, William Shakespeare recorded his version of the tragic tale of a Danish prince in dramatic format: *The Tragical History of Hamlet Prince of Denmark*. Commonly known as *Hamlet*, in this play the prince of Denmark is visited by the ghost of his recently deceased father, the former king. Like Odysseus's mother, this parent-spirit counsels his son. He cannot foresee the future, like the ghosts of *The Odyssey*, but he comes with a great purpose: to report that he was secretly murdered by his own brother. Hamlet's initial reaction to the ghost is to dismiss it as a wicked deception, a dark force conjured up by the devil. At the outset, his friends assume that the encounter is a manifestation of Hamlet's mental instability, but ultimately it becomes clear to the characters and the audience alike that this ghost is the real thing. For Shakespeare's audiences, ghosts were a plausible threat, and not limited to the realm of fantasy (Shakespeare 2002).

Even in 1897, when Henry James was writing his famous ghost tale, *The Turn of the Screw*, there was still widespread superstition about ghosts among Western audiences. In the introduction to a critical case study of this novella, Peter G. Beidler reminds modern readers that "James launched *The Turn of the Screw* into a world that seriously investigated ghostly phenomena . . . [He was] undoubtedly interested in them, knew about scientific reports about them and was acquainted with men directly involved in such research" (in James 2004, 19).

The novella[5] tells the tale of a young governess charged with two children at a remote country estate. She has authority over not only the boy and girl, but also the servants and every aspect of running the estate. The children's parents have died and it is an uncle, living in London, who provides for them. Shortly after the governess arrives she begins to have visions of a man named Peter Quint, first on the tower and then peering into the window. This man has been dead for a year and she never met him in life. She also sees the ghost of Miss Jessel, the former governess. The new governess, the first-person narrator of the story, is convinced that these apparitions are evil forces coming to win the souls of the two children. The tension of the story is composed of the narrator's desperate attempt to save the children and convince the other servants of the threat.

Readers are never quite convinced, however, that the young governess is completely sane. She is an unreliable narrator. Is this story a psychological study of a young woman isolated in the country, with too much responsibility? Or is this a true ghost story, about potentially malign spirits?

This debate has been brewing for quite some time within the ongoing critical discourse of Henry James's work. James is famous for his use of ambiguity, which is probably one of the reasons his work was included as a featured book in *Lost*, a show that lends itself to multiple interpretations. The suspenseful ending brings about the death of the little boy, Miles, in the arms of the governess. The reader never knows if the child actually sees the ghost and dies of fright, as the narrator claims, or if the governess strangles him to death, an even more terrifying possibility.

Lost's ghosts

In *Lost* there are several ghostly apparitions and, similar to Henry James's ghosts, their existence is ambiguous. For instance, precisely what is Jack's vision of Christian Shephard? At first it truly seems like a ghost, but then Jack points out that it could very easily be a hallucination brought on by the heat and the stress under which he is laboring. But later it is revealed that Christian's coffin is empty. Is it possible that he is some sort of zombie? Or is he a manifestation of the Smoke Monster? — though the Smoke Monster later admits that he took the form of Christian on the island, who was the man that Jack saw in the hospital off the island ("Something Nice Back Home"). This specter recalls both Odysseus's mother and Hamlet's father, spirits returning to their children to deliver a warning and a call to action. However, like modern-day readers of *The Turn of the Screw*, Jack cannot interpret this visitation as anything but the resulting hallucination of a stressful situation and a compromised mind. In the early stages of his developing character, he does not have the faith to believe or the eyes to see anything beyond the material life. It is clear, in any case, that the writers of *Lost* intentionally blur the line between supernatural and psychological explanations of the ghosts.

Hurley: from unreliable narrator to ghost whisperer

Hurley's initial experience with ghosts is similar to that of the narrator in *The Turn of the Screw*. He fears the apparitions at first and tries to ignore them. The audience, in turn, does not trust Hurley's visions, especially in light of the episode "Dave," which reveals Hurley to be mentally unstable and capable of conjuring up completely imaginary people. But it turns out that Hurley can actually communicate with people beyond the grave. When he encounters Charlie at the Santa Rosa Mental Institute, Charlie says, "I am dead but I'm also here" ("The Beginning of the End"). Hurley also has conversations with Eko, Ana Lucia and Jacob after they have died. Jacob, in fact, becomes very much like the ghost of Hamlet's father, frequently guiding Hurley in the right direction. Other apparitions include Michael, Yemi, Libby, Ben's mother and Isabella Alpert. In season six, the spirit of Michael makes it perfectly clear to Hurley that many of these souls are not ready to "move on," but since the Smoke Monster has the ability to take on different human forms, the line between ghost and optical illusion becomes blurry.

The nature of reality: mind games and madness

One of the more interesting aspects of the Dharma Initiative's work is their psychological and behavioral experimentation. Before they are wiped out by the Others, this group of scientists presumably initiates large-scale tests in behaviorism similar to B. F. Skinner's work. Some experiments are simply designed to see how well people respond to authority and to what extent subjects will follow instructions. In both the Pearl and the Swan stations, viewers see evidence of this kind of experimentation. One subject is ordered to enter a set of numbers into the computer every 108 minutes; another subject is instructed to observe this button-pusher on surveillance cameras and then record the findings. In the episode titled "Room 23" another, more sinister, dimension of the Dharma Initiative's innovative work is revealed. As punishment, or rehabilitation — it is never made clear — a character named Karl is taken to a room where he is strapped to a chair and forced to watch a psychedelic assortment of images and text on a large television screen, the sound of loud techno-rave music blaring into his headphones. This idea is an obvious reference to the conditioning scene in the Stanley Kubrick film *A Clockwork Orange*, based on the novel by Anthony Burgess (in McDowell 1983). The brainwashing images, however, are mostly ordinary, peaceful scenes from everyday life, nothing like the sadistic pictures in Kubrick's film. The messages, though, speak to the behavioral changes that presumably concerned the Dharma Initiative. They also address the psychological issues with which many of the characters grapple. "Everything changes," "we are the causes of our own suffering" and "God loves you as he loved Jacob" are the lines most relevant to the narrative. It is not clear how the Dharma Initiative originally designed the administration of the conditioning techniques, but it is apparent that they were interested in finding solutions to behavioral issues.

This "innovative" research brings to mind a particular theory about *Lost* based on the premise that all of the characters are more or less mentally ill. Marc Oromaner, author of the *Myth of Lost*, has speculated that the entire island narrative is a computer-generated simulation to "treat those with mental and behavioral disorders" (Oromaner 2008, 47) He conjectures that, given the mental instability of the characters, they willingly entered the program and were injected with false memories to explain how they arrived on the island. This theory would undoubtedly explain why so many criminal minds (Sawyer, Kate, Sayid, Ana Lucia, Eko, Jin) and addicts (Charlie, Hurley, Jack) are found among the castaways. According to Oromaner, Kate has the most serious psychological issues: she killed her father, drugged (and left) her husband and shot her boyfriend (63). Similarly, Sawyer is on a path of destruction and self-destruction when he comes to the island. More highly functioning characters are Jack and John, but both have histories of obsessive behavior, each suffering from a fixation on their fathers' approval.

Madness, magic and god

VALIS

This science-fiction novel by Philip K. Dick reflects the author's own mental breakdown and strange, religious visions. Among these visions is a pink beam of light that helps the main character, Horselover Fat, communicate with a spiritual entity, revealing all sorts of cosmic "truths" including the idea that we are all living in a time loop. Horselover Fat believes that there are actually two universes — the one that everyone can see and another, perceived only by the enlightened (Dick 1981). It has been argued that this book was greatly influential on the Wachowski brothers, creators of the film *The Matrix*, which also used elements of Lewis Carroll's works to convey certain themes.

VALIS depicts the disintegration of one man's mental faculties as he struggles to find the truth through his visions. Dick presents his readers with a religious quest embedded in science-fiction terms. This type of journey, fueled by madness, is not unlike John Locke's story. Locke has been gifted with a moment of truth, he has "looked into the eye of this island" and he is ready to do its bidding. The smoke can be compared to Horselover Fat's mystical pink beam of light. Similarly, Desmond Hume is haunted by visions and, like Horselover Fat, he frantically attempts to take action based on what he sees. Even after he has left the island, he is visited by a lucid memory in the form of a dream. This vision sends him, once again, doing the work of the island, the religious centerpiece of the entire series.

"Colonel Bloody Kurtz"

An excerpt of dialogue from the film *Apocalypse Now*, a movie loosely based on Joseph Conrad's *Heart of Darkness*, presents an explicit study of the struggle between good and evil. Before General Corman sends Willard on his mission to find Colonel Kurtz, a man engaging in horrendous acts of violence against the native people, he warns the soldier about the limits of the human spirit: "There's conflict in every human heart between the rational and the irrational, between good and evil. The good does not always triumph. Sometimes the dark side overcomes what Lincoln called the better angels of our nature. Every man has got a breaking point . . . Walter Kurtz has reached his. And very obviously he has gone insane" (Coppola 1979).

This passage offers a provocative definition of the notion of evil — it is not much different from insanity, beyond the pale of anything rational. Is this what the Smoke Monster embodies? Pure madness? In the season six episode "Across the Sea," viewers wonder who is actually crazy: Jacob, the mother, the Man in Black, or all of them? The episode illustrates what viewers already suspect to be true — that good and evil have no clear boundaries and that "darkness" is not inextricably linked to one character or another. But we do know that Claire, for instance, has been left in the wilderness and reached her "breaking point," which eventually compels her to commit callous acts of violence. Sayid is pushed over the edge by a great sense of loss and the inability to forgive himself. His desperation and loneliness nudge his spirit toward insanity and, ultimately, a sort of "zombification." Perhaps the Smoke Monster's plan works this way: the more "mad souls" that he recruits, the stronger he becomes. He continually deceives the islanders by directly lying to them or misguiding them with false entities that act and look like real people.

Indeed, the ghosts of *Lost* are a mixture of hallucination, island sorcery and supernatural spirits. It makes sense that Ben was steered in a very wrong direction by the Smoke Monster and that Jack doubted the magic of the island; the story's peculiar and unnatural occurrences find their origin in various sources, from the hallucinatory to the mystical. It also follows that viewers were confused by the quality and source of the mystery. The nature of reality in this world transcends genre, drawing from a collection of diverse narratives that attempt to explain uncanny phenomena. First, the series maintains a strong sense of sacred texts and classic literary works that rely on religious motifs. In these stories, disembodied spirits frequently return to interact with the living (*The Odyssey*, *Hamlet*). But *Lost* also models itself according to the psychological drama form, in which the protagonist's own mind becomes the monster (*The Turn of the Screw*, *Heart of Darkness*). Fantasy and dream narratives also play their parts in the making of this reality, with works like *Alice's Adventures in Wonderland* and *The Great Divorce* influencing the island narrative.

7

"Maybe There Is a Beast ... Maybe It's Only Us": Group Dynamics and the Communities of *Lost*

Many cities he saw and learned their minds / many pains he suffered, heartsick on the open sea, / fighting to save his life and bring his comrades home. / But he could not save them from disaster, hard as he strove — / the recklessness of their own ways destroyed them all.

— Homer (The Odyssey *1996, 77*)

Violence and social unrest

A Tale of Two Cities

The title of season three's premier episode, "A Tale of Two Cities," evokes a gruesome period in European history. The Charles Dickens novel for which the episode is named is set during the French Revolution and dramatizes "The Reign of Terror," a violent uprising of revolutionary fervor in France. In what is considered to be his only overtly political novel, Dickens reveals the French aristocracy of the late eighteenth century as deserving of the explosive social unrest. He illustrates their corruption of power and the unjust oppression of the masses. However, he is by no means sympathetic to the "degraded savages" who carried out the slaughter of the noblemen. In an essay simply titled "Charles Dickens" George Orwell argues that, "Revolution as [Dickens] sees it is merely a monster that is begotten by tyranny and always ends by devouring its own instruments" (Orwell 1991, 69).

Featured at the beginning of a new season, the borrowed title suggests that there has been a fundamental shift in the narrative of *Lost*. A new dynamic is introduced as the nature of the other society on the island becomes apparent. It appears that the Others maintain a well-established and highly developed social system. Rather than the barefoot "savages" the viewers once assumed them to be, this group has material riches, advanced knowledge and technology, and supreme control over the island. They are the all-powerful aristocracy of the island. But, like the French ruling class of the 1870s, if they oppress and abuse the castaways too much, they risk being destroyed by the "peasantry." Thus, the Smoke Monster, still an elusive specter at this point in the series, becomes a metaphor for the conflict between these two communities and the potential for violence that we see played out in subsequent seasons. The destructive acts of the castaways, from the capture and torture of "Henry Gale," to the gory axe murder of an Other by Claire in season six, remind viewers of the general tendencies of humans to rely on violence as a means of social organization, recalling the images set forth in Dickens' novel. "Dickens *is* very sure that the revolution is a monster," Orwell explains, "Again and again he insists upon the meaningless horrors of the revolution — the mass butcheries, the injustice, the ever-present terror of spies, the frightful blood-lust of the mob" (69).

Lord of the Flies

In William Golding's novel, *Lord of the Flies*, nuclear war is presumably responsible for the characters' predicament and the story's setting. While being ferried out of England and flown to a safer location, dozens of schoolboys find themselves on an uninhabited island when their plane crashes. No adults survive the disaster and the boys quickly begin organizing a micro-society, complete with an elected leader. Inevitably, the fragile order begins to crumble, intensified by one boy's provocations, and the few established rules fall away. Under these unstable conditions, the agitator, Jack, seizes power in dictator-like fashion. He uses food to control his subjects, organizing and ritualizing "the hunt," and claiming it as his own.

Lost is an obvious descendant of *Lord of the Flies*. Golding's narrative includes plane crash survivors, an island cut off from the rest of society, a "beast" in the jungle and the ongoing struggle to find a way home. But the narratives' most significant commonality is the fact that both islands serve as microcosms of a larger world. In *Lord of the Flies*, the boys' conflicts mirror the large-scale war raging over their home island of England and the important players responsible for the violence. Though the communities of *Lost* illustrate a wider range of life, they also reflect the distinguishing qualities of human interaction and group structure that inform international politics and the causes of war.

When Golding first published his book in the 1950s, threats of global war and nuclear devastation were fresh in the minds of his readers. Likewise, when *Lost* first aired in 2004, the threat of terrorism was new to many Western viewers. The US "war on terrorism" had recently been initiated and the images of destruction caused both by terrorist groups and "legitimate" acts of war were everywhere. The initial conflicts of the show — a devastating plane crash, the subsequent instability that followed and an unknown "monster" lurking beyond the threshold of community life — served as a fitting allegory for the post-9/11 era in the United States.

In general, *Lord of the Flies* warns its readers of the potential for human cruelty and destruction. In interviews, William Golding has admitted to a belief in the concept of original sin. Speaking to John Carey in 1986 he said, "I still think that the root of our sin is in there, in the child. As soon as it has any capacity for acting on the world outside, it will be selfish, and, of course, original sin and selfishness — the words could be interchangeable" (in Carey 1986, 175). Golding believed that people rely on certain aspects of civilization in order to keep their malevolent tendencies at bay. In *Lost*, this pessimistic position on human nature is reflected in the Man in Black's perspective, which he expresses to Jacob as they spot a ship approaching their shore: "They come, they corrupt, they destroy. It always ends the same" ("The Incident"). This statement is fitting for the boys in *Lord of the Flies*. Their innocence is corrupted once they realize they are released from the constraints of parental authority — they physically destroy their environment and each other, burning down much of the island (by neglecting their fire) and, ultimately, hunting and murdering the boys outside of the dominant group. One *Lord of the Flies* character, Simon, shares the gift of foresight with *Lost*'s Man in Black. Simon is unable to articulate his prophecy, but he seems to understand the hearts and minds of his fellow castaways and knows that their violent tendencies and mob mentality will ultimately destroy him.

Defining the monster

I shouted out / "Who killed the Kennedys?" / When after all, / It was you and me.
> — The Rolling Stones, "Sympathy for the Devil"

An important scene in *Lord of the Flies* takes place during an emergency assembly called by "chief" Ralph. This is a turning point in the story, where the tension gains momentum as the authority of the rules quickly begins to falter. Jack, the leader of the hunters, and the less democratic of the two, begins to rear his anarchical tendencies by publicly questioning Ralph's leadership. "Rules? Bollocks to the rules!" he shouts (Golding 1954).

The conflict begins to escalate during the boys' debate about the island's beast (or ghost). Unlike the Smoke Monster in *Lost*, this beast is decidedly a figment of the boys' collective imagination, at least from the reader's perspective. But the reality of its threat sharpens as each boy becomes more convinced of its existence. Fear of it, then, becomes a driving force behind the characters' motives. But Simon's comment reveals the beast for what it really is; he is the only one who understands its true nature and the very real threat it poses for the boys. Again, he plays the role of the prophet here, but his forewarning falls on deaf ears. As he takes the conch shell, a sign of authority and a cue for the other boys to listen, he feels a "perilous necessity to speak" (Golding 1954, 119):

> "Maybe," he said hesitantly, "maybe there is a beast."
>
> The assembly cried out savagely and Ralph stood up in amazement.
>
> "You, Simon? You believe in this?"
>
> "What I mean is . . . maybe it's only us."
>
> "Nuts!"
>
> That was from Piggy, shocked out of decorum. Simon went on.
>
> "We could be sort of . . ."
>
> Simon became inarticulate in his effort to express mankind's essential illness.

This last line, explanation directly from the narrator, given that Simon is unable to express himself, reveals everything we need to know about these castaways. Like all humans, they are self-destructive and capable of unspeakable acts of cruelty, especially in the face of fear. Quite simply, human instinct, left unchecked and multiplied by gang-like associations, is the most dangerous beast of all and yet these children are clearly blind to the danger.

Although the Smoke Monster actually materializes in corporeal form, *Lost*'s monster still has much in common with the imaginary beast of *Lord of the Flies*. For instance, Dogen describes the Smoke Monster as "evil incarnate," but it is Sayid who makes the decision to act out its wicked intentions. The Monster feeds on human weakness and "original sin." If he truly is "evil incarnate," he will only be destroyed when the other characters denounce his power and reclaim control over their lives.

To borrow from the idea that God dwells in every individual, one could say that the devil lives in each of us as well. A popular rendering of this figure, the Rolling Stones' "Sympathy for the Devil," characterizes the devil in a comparable fashion to the *Lord of the Flies* beast: "I rode the tank / held a general's rank / when blitzkrieg raged and the bodies stank." In other words, Satan or "the devil" witnessed the most gruesome atrocities of history because he was present inside all of its key players. There is no one individual evil entity — there is "only us."

Seizing power

A comparison of Jack, the young dictator from *Lord of the Flies*, and *Lost*'s Benjamin Linus reveals striking similarities between the group dynamics of both narratives, as the profile of a typical power-hungry leader emerges. Young Jack (*Lord of the Flies*) uses the illusion of exclusivity to gain power over the boys, slowly pulling their loyalty away from Ralph. By publicly recruiting certain boys he creates a sense of selectivity, but his ultimate goal is simply to control the largest number of subjects possible. In the same way, Ben Linus shrouds his purpose in mystery and draws in followers by convincing them that they are special. He is an expert at psychological manipulation, and his words are his most powerful tool. John Locke is the best example of a character influenced by Ben's rhetorical exploits.

In *Lord of the Flies* Jack makes a convincing case for his dictatorship, maintaining that if the other boys support him he will provide food and protection, but an even more pressing impetus is Jack's threat of violence. He is fervent about destroying all outsiders and develops a spectacle of brutality, ritualizing his militaristic system of governing with costume (war paint) and a rigid hierarchy of positions. Similarly, Ben uses fear to keep his followers in line by implementing a mysterious system of special codes, ritualistic protocol and an elaborate mythology. In the same way that Jack (*Lord of the Flies*) tests the boys by having them murder Simon, Ben tests John by making him kill his own father.

Probably the most significant shared characteristic of Ben and young Jack is their common tendency toward despotism. They are both responsible for overturning one system of government and supplanting it with their own. Viewers will recall Ben's genocidal actions against the Dharma Initiative, motivated by the promise of power. Similarly, Jack is determined to destroy any individual who threatens his tight grasp on a supreme leadership of the boys.

Ideas, ideals and ideology

The True Believer: Thoughts on the Nature of Mass Movements

In "Dr. Linus," an alternate version of Ben is presented to the audience. Dr. Benjamin Linus, a high school history teacher living in Los Angeles, delivers a lecture on the initial exile of Napoleon, explaining to his students that the French revolutionary was able to maintain his title of emperor, but might as well have been dead considering he was devoid of power without his subjects; he was isolated on the island of Elba. The inclusion of this bit of history here in the series suggests that even this version of Ben has the potential to become a fanatic revolutionary, if given a chance. But this episode also reminds viewers of Ben's status as a man of words. He has earned a doctorate in European History and he makes his living by reading, writing and delivering lectures. Like the original version of Ben, he uses words as weapons, convincing Leslie Arzt to side with him and attempting to displace the principal by blackmailing him with a stack of scandalous email correspondence.

In *The True Believer: Thoughts on the Nature of Mass Movements*, an analysis of fanaticism and the conditions that create social unrest, Eric Hoffer divides leaders of mass movements into three groups: Men of Words, Fanatics and Practical Men of Action. According to Hoffer the "articulate minority" initiates the first steps of a revolutionary movement. "Discrediting [the prevailing order] is not an automatic result of the blunders and abuses of those in power, but the deliberate work of men of words with a grievance" (130). Hoffer points out that the divisions he makes among these groups is not meant to be categorical. A Man of Words sometimes becomes a Fanatic or a Practical Man of Action. Most significant is that the Man of Words provides an effective call to action that the masses cannot ignore. "His appeal is usually to reason and not to faith. The fanatics and faith-hungry masses, however, are likely to invest such speculations with the certitude of holy writ and make them the fountainhead of a new faith" (140).

Benjamin Linus, Richard Alpert, Sawyer and the Smoke Monster are good examples of *Lost*'s Men of Words, each in their own way. In many cases, Ben has saved his own life and initiated a change using rhetoric alone. He talks his way out of captivity in the hatch, by convincing Michael to make a deal with him ("Two for the Road"), he persuades Jack to operate on his tumor ("The Cost of Living"), and he manipulates John into carrying out various questionable acts to "protect the island." The Smoke Monster (in the form of John Locke) also uses words alone to mobilize others. He convinces the whole group to follow him to the statue where he plans to murder Jacob ("Follow the Leader"), he persuades Sawyer to accompany him into the jungle ("The Substitute") and dissuades Sayid from killing him ("Sundown"). Even Dogen suggests that the Smoke Monster possesses extraordinary powers of language. He tells Sayid, "As soon as you see him, plunge this [dagger] deep into his chest. If you allow him to speak, it is already too late." Predictably, Sayid does allow him to speak first and the Smoke Monster is able to change Sayid's mind, appealing to his sense of desperation; further, he convinces Sayid to murder the very man who sent him — Dogen.

A less obvious Man of Words is found in the evolved character of James Ford, also known as Sawyer. In the episode "Namaste" Jack visits Sawyer (known as "LaFleur" at this point) in his cabin to ask about the Dharma folks capturing Sayid. When Jack admonishes Sawyer for not taking immediate action, Sawyer explains that he is a "thinker" and that he doesn't just explode into action at the slightest provocation. In the following lines Sawyer is seen wearing glasses and has a book on his lap as he sits in the quiet space of his living room, presumably modeling himself after a legendary war strategist:

Sawyer: I heard once Winston Churchill read a book every night, even during the Blitz. He said it made him think better. It's how I like to run things. I think. I'm sure that doesn't mean that much to you, 'cause back when you were calling the shots, you pretty much just reacted. See, you didn't think, Jack, and as I recall, a lot of people ended up dead.

Jack: I got us off the island.

Sawyer: But here you are . . . right back where you started. So I'm gonna go back to reading my book, and I'm gonna think, 'cause that's how I saved your ass today. And that's how I'm gonna save Sayid's tomorrow.

Unlike Ben and the Smoke Monster, Sawyer uses his heightened sense of literacy and his status as a "man of letters" for the benefit of others. But in either case, whether words are intended to harm or to help, these characters demonstrate what Hoffer articulates in his work: language plays a powerful role in any kind of social organization or group collaboration.

The True Believers, however, are the real troublemakers, according to Hoffer. "All mass movements generate in their adherents a readiness to die and a proclivity for united action; all of them demand blind faith and single-hearted allegiance." The island's relationship with its inhabitants represents the connection between dogma and the "true believer." John Locke and Ben Linus fit the definition of True Believers in relation to the island. Indeed, throughout the seasons we've seen many characters eager to sacrifice themselves, if not for the island, then at least for the "greater good." Most have a "proclivity for united action" as we see in their tendency to form exclusive groups and to demonize the Other (including, but not strictly defined by, "the Others").

Hoffer argues that the kind of person most likely to become an extremist, whether religious or political, is entirely frustrated by his inadequacy as an individual and will seize the first opportunity to relinquish his freedom for a larger cause. The characters of *Lost* repeatedly say things like, "I did it for the island," "the island will tell me what to do," "my [or your] purpose is to be on this island," and "it was for the island's sake." These characters renounce their individual lives back home and their personal freedom simply to be part of something larger. They are True Believers, each willing to replace individuality with a "holy cause."

Most of the characters, at one point or another in the narrative, exhibit a need to escape their individuality and the heavy burden of freedom that comes with it. The seemingly inexplicable motive for returning to the island is evidence of this common characteristic of the human condition. After the "Oceanic 6" are rescued, they lose the power of a unified purpose and the strong bond they formed as collaborative survivors. They no longer feel sufficient without the unifying purpose that comes with a group association.

Lost dramatizes the same destructive powers of fanaticism and blind discipleship that we see in real life, whether it is unethical behavior for the sake of a political party, or a war in the name of a set of religious values. As Ben tells Mikhail in "Through the Looking Glass, Part 1," "everything I did, I did for the island."

Utopias and dystopias: *Animal Farm, Lost Horizon* and *Island*

When Kate reveals that Jack is in charge of the case of guns in "Expose," Leslie Arzt suddenly becomes alarmed by the leadership roles that some characters are assuming. In his frustration at the self-ordained group of leaders (Jack, Kate, John and Hurley), Arzt utters an explicit reference to George Orwell's 1945 allegorical "beast fable": "the pigs are walking!"

Arzt's sentiment reflects the divisive forces at play in Orwell's satiric novel among the "citizens" of the newly organized Animal Farm, formerly known as Manor Farm. Led by a group of pigs, most notably Napoleon and Snowball, the animals revolt against the farmers and drive them out. They take control of the farm and establish their own community, governed by the Seven Commandments of Animalism. The first law states that "whatever goes upon two legs is an enemy." Thus, the accusation that "the pigs are walking" is a harsh condemnation of corrupt leadership. Eventually, a division grows between the two leaders and they disagree on the future of their community. Snowball wants to implement plans for an agrarian utopia, with the help of a windmill, but Napoleon is concerned about more practical issues and thinks the project is a waste of time. Eventually, the more tyrannical leader, Napoleon, resorts to violence to defend his position.

The Dharma Initiative's goals reflect the same utopian vision held by the fictional animals. Like the new farm, the Dharma community is destroyed by forces within the group and their idealistic theories, in practice, make for a dystopia. But Orwell's work can be revealed in other ways on the island. The Dharma group, for example, might be more closely associated with the farmers, and the Others to the farm animals. The dynamic among Orwell's characters is also reflected by the dichotomy between the survivors of the middle section and Ana Lucia's group from the tail section.

While *Animal Farm* warns against the pitfalls of applying prohibitively lofty ideals to the governing of a people, James Hilton's *Lost Horizon* offers an attractive vision of how an idyllic governing model might be successful. (See Chapter 2 for more on *Lost Horizon*). The community that Conway and his fellow castaways find in the Tibetan mountains offers a plausible portrait of utopia. The isolation of the community prevents the infiltration of corrupting forces, and the central values of moderation and anti-extremism inhibit the encouragement of fanatic leadership. The central protagonist of the story, Conway, finds the society to be quite amenable to his nature, but his young companion, Mallinson, is suspicious and scornful of the mysterious lamasery and its tranquil valley. The High Lama hopes that one day their society will serve as a guide to the rest of the world, a leader on the path to enlightenment.

However, it is never made clear whether the High Lama's plans are wholly benevolent. One of the residents tells Mallinson that she has been held there against her will; then, when she finally escapes Shangri-La her body instantaneously grows old and decays. One particularly suspicious aspect of the enchanted Himalayan village is that the four castaways were brought there against their own intentions and have no way of escaping. Although the authorities tell them they are free to go whenever they wish, they know that the rough terrain and freezing temperatures would make it impossible to survive without aid. Nature serves to imprison the characters in a seeming paradise, and this has its effect on the isolated society. Similarly, the survivors of the *Lost* plane crash are isolated, with no means of communicating with the outside world. But unlike *Lost Horizon*, they are met with hostile indifference when they arrive. The established society of the Others are not welcoming, nor will they permit the castaways to leave.

Aldous Huxley's final book, *Island*, demonstrates a strikingly similar setting to that of *Lost Horizon*, with its secluded location supporting a relatively serene society composed of emotionally balanced citizens. The novel is more rewarding when read as an exploration of utopian civilization rather than simply a story. It is littered with explanations about ideal solutions to political conflict and philosophical musings on scientific innovation and education. It explicitly grapples with issues of environmentalism, overpopulation, international politics, corruption of power and industrialization. Huxley seems to use his last novel to work through some of his earlier ideas about the dangers of the utopian vision, discovering a more finely tuned version of utopia in his fictitious island of Pala.

Pala is an island rich in oil and other valuable resources, and most of its inhabitants are concerned about the potential for outside parties of power, whether governmental or corporate, to exploit their home. They want to maintain the virginal wilderness of the land and the ideal vision of their society. However, the young Raja, Murugan, heir to the throne, has spent much of his youth away from the island and, according to the Palanese, his values have been polluted by Western ideas and the laws of capitalism. Ultimately he betrays them all, bowing to corporate interests as he makes a deal with a neighboring country that wants to take advantage of Pala's natural resources.

Before looking at *Island*'s more profound connections to the group dynamics of *Lost*, it would be helpful to examine some of the more superficial qualities that the novel shares with the television program. The book's opening and closing scenes are comparable to *Lost*'s mood and setting. The first paragraph describes a man opening his eyes after crashing on the island, which calls attention to *Lost*'s most pervading image: the opening of a single eye. This protagonist, Will Farnaby, props himself up on one elbow to see "a glade among trees and the long shadows and slanting lights of an early morning forest." Viewers will recall that the opening scene of *Lost*'s pilot episode features an identical setting, complete with "long shadows and slanting lights." Next, the narrative moves to a flashback, detailing the events of a painful relationship, and then brings the reader back to the present, in characteristically *Lost* format. The final scene of the book has an apocalyptic feel, as the island's inhabitants learn that the world as they know it is coming to an end. The outside world is closing in, as the "others" encroach and plan to occupy and exploit the island, destroying the Palanese way of life.

The history of the island's community dates back to the early nineteenth century when the Raja hired Dr. MacPhail, a British physician, to remove a tumor from his face. Dr. MacPhail's arrival on the island marks the confluence of Western science and Eastern spirituality, a central theme of this story. The Palanese people are able to appreciate the gifts of modern medicine and combine its practice with the mindfulness of Buddhism. This permutation recalls the Dharma Initiative's framework of Eastern-inspired titles, rituals and symbols within an organization based mostly on experimental Western science and technology (the use of the term "Namaste," the I Ching symbol, and the term "dharma"). Like the Dharma Initiative, the founders of Pala were interested in psychological experimentation in order to find a formula for producing emotionally wholesome human beings.

The Palanese are, indeed, quite successful at rearing spiritually and intellectually robust children and productive, well-behaved citizens. One of the converts to Palanese life, Dr. Robert, specializes in holistic remedies for problematic children. He separates the troubled kids into two categories: the Muscle Men and the Peter Pans. He considers the boy heir, Murugan, to be one of the latter. These are people, usually male, who do not develop well enough, emotionally, to deal with the responsibilities and challenges of adult life. They are always in a state of "retarded maturation." As children, they usually exhibit a refusal to learn and grow, and the inability to get along with others. As adults

"Peter Pans are wonderfully good at starting wars and revolutions" (187). They are the "mute inglorious Hitlers, the village Napoleons, the Calvins and Torquemadas" (182). But Dr. Robert has found a way to prevent these kinds of children, both the Muscle Men and the Peter Pans, from developing into frustrated, destructive adults. He prescribes "three pink pills a day," hard physical labor and regular meditation. In other words, he treats them with a little science, a little nature and a big dose of spirituality. For the Palanese, balance and temperance are the most important qualities of life. All inhabitants are encouraged to find and follow "the middle way."

Both the castaways and the Others could learn a lot from the Palanese about simply getting along with others and building a successful, if temporary, society. When the story of *Island* begins, the Palanese have already overcome many of the typical social problems by using psychological conditioning and spiritual practices that maintain peace. The Dharma Initiative never got that far. They were working on experiments to see how well people responded to authority and how far subjects would follow instructions based on faith alone. But it is really faith in other human beings that makes for a flourishing social structure. Characters like Ben, from *Lost*, and Murugan, from *Island*, lack the very important quality on which all human relationships rely: trust. We are formed only in relation to one another but we enter into relationships in a state of vulnerability and need. Some characters cannot seem to overcome their weaknesses and end up deceiving others and distrusting everyone, tearing the fabric of the community to shreds.

Redemption through community

One must be fond of people and trust them if one is not to make a mess of life.

— E. M. Forster

In Jean-Paul Sartre's existentialist drama *No Exit* (see more on *No Exit* in Chapter 2), three characters are stuck in a room together for all of eternity. One says to another: "If you make any movement, if you raise your hand to fan yourself, Estelle and I feel a little tug. Alone, none of us can save him or herself; we're linked together inextricably" (Sartre 1976, 29). This calls to mind Jack Shephard's pep talk in season one's "White Rabbit." He tells his fellow castaways that "if we can't live together, we're going to die alone." It is only when they acknowledge their interdependence that they can save themselves. In "Redemption on the Island of Second Chances," Brett Chandler Patterson describes the survivors' possibility for rebirth: "this opportunity for a new start, for a second chance, arrives primarily in becoming a part of a community of survivors. The story reminds us that our identities largely arise in our relationships with those around us" (Patterson 2008, 216).

When the castaways of *Lost* realize there is no escape from the island, their group dynamic begins to change. Days after the initial plane crash, many of them recognize that they need to focus their energies on surviving rather than wasting time trying to get rescued. Naturally, there is a disagreement about this and the group splits into two camps, one on the beach and one in the jungle. It is interesting to note here that they begin referring to each group as "the other" until they encounter an outside force — the *real* Others — which unifies them once again. When Michael's boat is set on fire they blame one another, but John Locke quickly points out that they are not alone on the island, and once again they unite against the unknown entity lurking beyond the threshold of their community. When Desmond returns on his boat, after realizing he can't escape, he tells the group, "We are stuck in a bloody snow globe! There's no outside world. There's no escape" ("Live Together, Die Alone"). The idea that they are all trapped together indeterminably primes the group for the next stage in the development of their society. Recognition that there is "no exit" from the island stimulates a sense of group cooperation.

In *Lost* the characters' capacity to emotionally connect with one another and to develop a functional community can make the difference between salvation and damnation. We might attribute this theme to the famous message in *The Brothers Karamazov*, "all are responsible for all." Father Zossima, Alyosha Karamazov's monastic elder, claims that "There is only one means of salvation, then take yourself and make yourself responsible for all men's sins . . . for as soon as you make yourself responsible for everything and for all men, you will see at once that it is really so, that you are to blame for everyone and all things" (310). This is the lesson of *The Brothers Karamazov*, that we are not only responsible for the whole of humanity but also guilty of the collective crimes. The novel also poses countless other moral questions about social and emotional engagement: How much are we responsible for the suffering of others? Why is life designed in such a way that men can easily hurt one another? Why are human beings so weak and corruptible? Is free will worth the damage that we inflict on others and that others inevitably inflict upon us?

Despite the potential for corruption among social organizations and their leaders, the characters in all of the stories mentioned in this chapter, like all human beings, are naturally interdependent. That communities are necessary for the human race to flourish is an obvious point, but the message seems to get lost in the solitary mode of living in which many modern-day people conduct their lives. The characters in *Lost* are participants in an extraordinary community, a microcosm of a larger society, and they work collectively to shift the paradigm of the island and, arguably, they affect the fate of the world. In the end (or "The End"), everyone who cooperated and sacrificed themselves for the group was redeemed. They achieved a sort of salvation by reassembling the group in the afterlife and remembering in communion, reflecting on the significance of their lives together. Redemption through community is the most important message of the *Lost* series, from Jack's "live together, die alone" speech in season one to the significance of togetherness in the resolution of the final episode.

In this context, it makes sense that Hurley has been chosen as the new protector of the island. He understands that cooperation and collaborative effort for the sake of the group can elevate the human spirit. It is fitting that one of his first tasks on the island is to sort out and distribute the food to all of the castaways. He also creates a golf course on the island for the sole purpose of strengthening the union of the community, bringing them together and easing their tension. He clearly maintains strong attachments to others, which proves to be more important than sustaining a special connection to the island. The series' inherent message is that social connection and emotional engagement are the keys to redemption and a "life after death." Christian tells Jack that all of his friends have come together "to remember." They have constructed a shared space together, even in the spiritual world, to illustrate that "no one does it alone." These characters gather to create a place for their own salvation, even if being saved is simply a matter of "letting go."

8

Conclusion: The Purpose of "Stories That Aren't Even True"

Characters on Lost, *like the characters in* Battlestar [Galactica] *are addressing a fundamental question which is "How do I get home?" ... And what is the meaning of home? And that's the question of* The Odyssey, *it's the question of the Exodus story, it's the question of the* Wizard of Oz. *I think it's a question that all of us have.*
— *Diane Winston* (TV and Parables of Our Time *2009*)

Collectively, the works of literature with which *Lost* associates itself create a metanarrative, a self-commentary that helps viewers gain a broader understanding of the show's plot devices, characters and themes. In one fell swoop, for instance, a reference to Kurt Vonnegut's novel *Slaughterhouse-Five* reveals a number of things about the show: it acknowledges *Lost's* rootedness in other science-fiction cult narratives, it initiates a discussion of free will, and it draws attention to the absurdity of human violence. Sacred narratives are especially helpful in the interpretation of *Lost*, with passages and images that provide clear cultural reference points for understanding notions of redemption, sacrifice, faith and a vision of the afterlife. Allusions to other stories, such as *Alice's Adventures in Wonderland* and *The Wonderful Wizard of Oz* provide larger-than-life characters and settings that serve to enlarge the viewers' imaginative scope and add fantastic potentialities to the narrative. Paying homage to such works as Golding's *Lord of the Flies* and Conrad's *Heart of Darkness* emphasizes the social and psychological difficulties of the human condition, while *Watership Down* and *The Brothers Karamazov* underscore the message that cooperative collaboration and community-building are valuable agents for the salvation of human life.

The general objective of this book is to enrich the viewing experience of *Lost* by using literary works of fiction as companion texts;

it also endeavors to position the series within the context of a wider tradition of narratives. I hope that it can also provide a unique mode of revitalizing works of literature in educational settings, whether classrooms or less formal learning environments like book clubs. Perhaps this text can help broaden viewers' appreciation of the potential for television to inspire engagement in other narrative formats by acknowledging the significance of "intertextuality" in this series. Countless fans of *Lost* have found that the literary allusions have broadened their viewing experience and I anticipate that other television narratives can have the same effect, while still maintaining the integrity of the primary narrative.

Finding meaning: the importance of "something to think about"

Among the chatter that ensued throughout the final season on blogs, discussion boards, Facebook, and other countless venues, the following sentiment loomed large: "What am I going to think about when the series ends?" This concern is understandable; for me, especially, it seems that the final season consisted of nothing but critical analysis of the show — discussion in my courses, scribblings in my "Lost and Literature" blog and, naturally, writing this book. To be sure, *Lost* is responsible for many a dynamic debate, usually involving a diverse group of contributors from various parts of the world. In an age of widespread digital social interaction, a good television narrative is one that can sustain a sense of community. A successful television program poses questions fit for a collective voice, a vigilant audience of active participants. The shared social construct of the *Lost* text is what makes this series so distinctly appealing, and fans will likely miss the discussions almost as much as the show. So the question should not be "What am I going to think about?" but, rather, "What am I going to think about in the company of other thinkers?"

A good portion of this book argues that the notion of community is a vital key in *Lost*, but this argument can operate on more than one level. Within the narrative, the idea is clearly evident — redemption, salvation and even the construction of memories rely on a sense of communion with others — but evidence of social convergence outside of the text is also abundant. The six-year event of *Lost* has benefited from the cohesive nature of its audience, a network of active viewers who contribute to a vast database of collective information, helping one another understand the show and unearth greater meaning. Fans' enjoyment of the show is not strictly limited to the story; rather it is the shared experience of a narrative (including shared theories and analyses) that allows viewers to recall and comprehend such a long and meandering plot. Collectively, *Lost* fans have enjoyed the ability to unravel the intricate narrative threads, while expanding the story with their own interpretations and compelling questions.

Consider the fan base of *Lost* in light of the narrative's inherent message that social collaboration and emotional engagement are the keys to redemption and a "life after death." By extension, I argue that remembering "in communion" provides an afterlife for the series, allowing fans to serve as protectors of the "source of all life," to use an analogy originating from the island narrative. Going forward, fans will rely on each other to assemble a complete memorial of the story, which is reflected in the thousands of fan sites, blogs and "*Lost* events," but also dramatized in the finale. Christian tells Jack that all of his friends have come together "to remember"; they have constructed a shared space together. In the same way, no reader of fiction or viewer of television and film understands the story in isolation. Readers approach canonical works of literature accompanied by a tradition of critical interpretation and viewers of television rely on the ongoing discourse of professional entertainment journalists, bloggers and fan boards. In the words of Christian Shephard, "no one does it alone."

Many of us spend our darkest days and most joyous moments physically closed off from the larger community, sometimes forgetting our emotional obligations to others. Taking into consideration the books referenced in *Lost*, viewers can see that the show's writers are touching upon something profound — that humans are utterly alone, in solitary confinement both physically and spiritually. We are perpetually "Other" to one another, never able to fully trust or completely empathize with those who are external to the self. And yet, we are inextricably linked and frequently saved, touched and transformed by others. We are alone but we are also connected to the rest of humanity in vital ways. *Of Mice and Men*, for instance, one work that has received considerable coverage on the show, is a short novel by John Steinbeck about the ills and inevitability of loneliness, but also about the deep connections that humans have the potential to forge. *The Brothers Karamazov* underscores man's ability to inflict grief and pain upon one another and the influence, whether positive or negative, that we have on one another. We are all responsible or "are guilty for all." *Watership Down* demonstrates the interdependence of life and addresses the notion that sometimes salvation is found in the most unlikely sources of life. Though the novel is "about bunnies," the humanity that the characters exhibit, and their ability to reach across the aisle to other species in order to "live together," serves as a model for creating a valuable human community.

The role of fiction, the purpose of *Lost*

To borrow an often-used analogy in the community of *Lost* viewers, we have all crash-landed into this existence and do not know what's beyond "the island." We are never given a clear idea about why we are here, and cleaning up the "wreckage" into which we are born seems hopeless and sometimes even dangerous. *Lost* demonstrates this condition in explicit terms, dramatizing the very essence of the central human concern: to find a purpose. In this island narrative, each individual is boiled down to his or her essential elements, stripped of the accoutrements of his or her pre-island life. They all must work together with what they are given; they have to face one another and, in the reflection of each other, discover their true selves.

Azar Nafisi, author of the memoir *Reading Lolita in Tehran*, once paid a visit to my university and I was fortunate enough to have her as a guest in my classroom. One of the things she discussed with my students was the role of fiction in our lives and, to quote Salman Rushdie's *Haroun and the Sea of Stories* (another *Lost* book), to understand the significance of stories that "are not even true." What is the point of fiction in our daily lives? Nafisi answers this question pointedly in her memoir: "A great novel heightens your senses and sensitivity to the complexities of life and of individuals, and prevents you from the self-righteousness that sees morality in fixed formulas about good and evil" (Nafisi 2003, 133). Certainly, *Lost* is not a "great novel" — indeed, it is not a novel at all — but I think most viewers would agree that it does pass the test of good storytelling, in the sense that it has "heightened our senses and sensitivity" and that it has been guarded about judging its characters, careful to stay away from "fixed formulas" of morality. *Lost* allows its viewers to identify with a diverse community of people struggling with basic human problems and learning to connect with one another. Most viewers would agree that it has pushed its audience to interpret aspects of their own lives in a new light, just like any good (written) story would do. In fact, many fans have made claims such as, "*Lost* has changed my life" or "*Lost* has altered my perspective of the world." Certainly these remarks count for something in the assessment of *Lost*'s success as a quality narrative.

If literature is meant "to instruct and delight"[1] as the ancient Roman poet Horace once claimed and countless literature teachers have repeated since, then why should other modes of fiction not be expected to "instruct" or attempt to challenge the viewer on an intellectual level? Cynics have claimed that television is a mildly entertaining diversion at best, but that it offers little or no redeeming qualities (usually with the implication that there is little potential for this medium's transformation). I will not endeavor to tackle this argument here, but it strikes me that one should not throw out the medium with the bathwater of bad programming. Indeed, there are plenty of shows that provide little value, but *Lost* is in good company within a new generation of television that continues to improve the artistic worth of the medium. Like *Lost,* these newer programs, such as *Mad Men, Breaking Bad* and *The Wire* are not perfect, but they demonstrate the potential of the television program, a form of narrative long admonished for its "dumbing down" of viewers. They "instruct" in the sense that a well-written work of literature has the potential to teach the reader about the complexity of moral conflict or to illustrate an empathetic rendering of the Other. They do this indirectly, all the while focusing on the aspects that entertain and "delight" the audience. The didacticism of *Lost*'s literary allusions work in quite the same way; they provide a context for certain works of literature, implicitly inviting the viewer to become a reader of literary fiction, and simultaneously "delighting" the audience by identifying stories with which they are already familiar. The metanarrative will continue to instruct long after the series has ended as fans continue to read works of literature based on the suggestions of the show's writers. Thus, *Lost*'s instruction and its entertainment are inextricable.

Appendix
List of Literary Allusions

The following is a list of books that have been directly referenced in the show.

After All These Years, Susan Isaacs
Alice's Adventures in Wonderland, Lewis Carroll
Animal Farm, George Orwell
Are You There God? It's Me, Margaret, Judy Blume
Bad Twin, Gary Troup
Beyond Freedom and Dignity, B. F. Skinner
Bluebeard, Charles Perrault
A Brief History of Time: From the Big Bang to Black Holes, Stephen Hawking
The Brothers Karamazov, Fyodor Dostoevsky
Captain Gault, Being the Exceedingly Private Log of a Sea-Captain, William Hope Hodgson
Caravan of Dreams, Idries Shah
Carrie, Stephen King
Catch-22, Joseph Heller
The Chosen, Chaim Potok
A Christmas Carol, Charles Dickens
The Chronicles of Narnia, C. S. Lewis
The Coalwood Way, Homer Hickam
Dark Horse, Tami Hoag
Deep River, Shūsaku Endō
Dirty Work, Stuart Woods
The Epic of Gilgamesh
Everything That Rises Must Converge, Flannery O'Connor
Evil Under the Sun, Agatha Christie
Fahrenheit 451, Ray Bradbury
Fear and Trembling, Søren Kierkegaard
Flowers for Algernon, Daniel Keyes

The Fountainhead, Ayn Rand
The Great Divorce, C. S. Lewis
Haroun and the Sea of Stories, Salman Rushdie
Harry Potter, J. K. Rowling
Heart of Darkness, Joseph Conrad
High Hand, Gary Phillips
Hindsight, Peter Wright
The Holy Bible
The Holy Qur'an
Hotel, Arthur Hailey
The Invention of Morel, Adolfo Bioy Casares
Island, Aldous Huxley
The Island of Dr. Moreau, H. G. Wells
Julius Caesar, William Shakespeare
Jurassic Park, Michael Crichton
Kings of Love: The Poetry and History of the Ni'matullahi Sufi Order,
      Pūrjavādī, Nasrollah and Peter Lamborn Wilson (translators)
Lancelot, Walker Percy
Laughter in the Dark, Vladimir Nabokov
Left Behind, Tim LaHaye and Jerry Jenkins
The Little Prince, Antoine de Saint-Exupery
Lord of the Flies, William Golding
Lost Horizon, James Hilton
Manservant and Maidservant, Ivy Compton-Burnett
Memoirs of a Geisha, Arthur Golden
Moby Dick, Herman Melville
The Moon Pool, Abraham Merritt
Mysteries of the Ancient Americas: The New World before Columbus,
      Reader's Digest Staff
The Mysterious Island, Jules Verne
Notes From Underground, Fyodor Dostoevsky
The Oath, John Lescroart
An Occurrence at Owl Creek Bridge, Ambrose Bierce
The Odyssey, Homer
Of Mice and Men, John Steinbeck
On the Road, Jack Kerouac
On Writing, Stephen King
Our Mutual Friend, Charles Dickens
The Outsiders, S. E. Hinton
The Pearl, John Steinbeck
Rainbow Six, Tom Clancy

Rick Romer's Vision of Astrology, Rick Romer
Robinson Crusoe, Daniel Defoe
Roots, Alex Haley
A Separate Reality, Carlos Castaneda
The Shape of Things to Come, H. G. Wells
The Sheltering Sky, Paul Bowles
The Shining, Stephen King
Slaughterhouse-Five, Kurt Vonnegut
The Stand, Stephen King
The Stone Leopard, Colin Forbes
Stranger in a Strange Land, Robert Heinlein
The Survivors of the Chancellor, Jules Verne
A Tale of Two Cities, Charles Dickens
The Tempest, William Shakespeare
The Third Policeman, Flann O'Brien
Through the Looking-Glass and What Alice Found There, Lewis
  Carroll
Tibetan Book of the Dead
To Kill a Mockingbird, Harper Lee
The Turn of the Screw, Henry James
Ulysses, James Joyce
Uncle Tom's Cabin, Harriet Beecher Stowe
Valhalla Rising, Clive Cussler
VALIS, Philip K. Dick
Watership Down, Richard Adams
The Wonderful Wizard of Oz, L. Frank Baum
A Wrinkle in Time, Madeleine L'Engle

Notes

Introduction

1. Henry Jenkins explains the notion of "participatory culture" in more than one publication, including *Convergence Culture: Where Old and New Media Collide* (NYU Press, 2006).

2. For example, the mention of the name "Colonel Kurtz," refers to the film *Apocalypse Now* but it implies the character simply named "Kurtz" of Joseph Conrad's classic novella, *Heart of Darkness*.

3. The term intertextuality is a problematic one because of its divergent meanings. It has been widely interpreted in a number of ways by theorists in different fields. It works here as a term that connotes a simple "interconnectedness" of a wide variety of texts. "The act of reading, theorists claim, plunges us into a network of textual relations. To interpret a text, to discover its meaning or meanings, is to trace those relations" (Allen 2000).

4. Michelle Lang explores this notion in "*Lost* as the Neo-Baroque," an essay featured on the "Lost Studies" website, also known as "The Society for the Study of Lost." David Lavery has also applied Ndalianis's neo-baroque model to *Lost*.

5. The following websites support book club communities: "LOST Books Challenge" and the "Master Lost Book List."

6. This class, based on the "*Lost*-centric" media studies writing courses that I developed at the University of North Florida, was held for a six-week session in the summer of 2009, between seasons five and six. I designed it with fans in mind and opened it to the public.

Chapter 1

1. Colonel Kurtz is a character in the 1979 film *Apocalypse Now*, which is loosely based on *Heart of Darkness*.

2. Indeed, this classic story (*The Odyssey*) is a hero's journey or "monomyth," as romantically defined by Joseph Campbell. It has been argued that *Lost*, along with other mass media "parables," also fits the monomyth construct (*Star Wars* and *The*

Matrix, to name the big titles). Campbell has created a set of characteristics that make up any hero's journey: the Departure, which includes the Call to Adventure, the Refusal of the Call, the Supernatural Aid, the Crossing of the First Threshold and the Belly of the Whale. Then there is the Initiation, which is made up of The Road of Trials, The Meeting with the Goddess, Woman as Temptress, Atonement with the Father, Apotheosis and The Ultimate Boon. Lastly, the return of the hero consists of the following phases: the Refusal of the Return, The Magic Flight, Rescue from Without, the Crossing of the Return Threshold, Master of the Two Worlds and Freedom to Live.

Chapter 2

1. Considering that the directive to regularly monitor the computer comes directly out of a bible (the book used as a vessel for the Orientation tape), Jack's rejection of it is fitting.

Chapter 3

1. An extensive commentary of *The Brothers Karamazov* can be found in Chapter 5.

2. This image recalls the "shoes of destiny" in season five — Jack puts Christian's shoes on the corpse of John Locke. The shoes seem to possess a mystical power and are presented as essential in bringing the body of Locke to the Smoke Monster.

[3]This is a reference to Joseph Campbell's "monomyth" or hero's journey. For more on the monomyth see discussion on *The Odyssey* in note 2 for Chapter 1.

4. I address the possibility of Billy Pilgrim's mental illness in greater depth in Chapter 4, "Stuck and 'Unstuck' in Time."

5. Island dwellers Richard and Jacob also enjoy extended lives.

6. One of John Locke's signal phrases is "We were brought here for a reason, for a purpose."

7. For one, Jessica Engelking discusses the connections in the *Lost and Philosophy* chapter, "*Lost*, *The Third Policeman* and Guerilla Ontology." David Lavery, Lynetter Porter and Hillary Robson also address the book's influence in *Lost's Buried Treasures*.

Chapter 4

1. It is not simply the segment of the audience that self-identifies as science-fiction fans who benefit from the incorporation of time travel.

2. A Minkowski space is a representation of space–time as a cube. It was named for the scientist Herman Minkowski. George Minkowski, a character from season

four's freighter, dies from complications of time travel. In season six this scientist's name arises again in physicist Daniel Faraday's drawing of the Minkowski-Einstein equation.

Chapter 5

1. "The Colossus" is another of Plath's poetic treatments of the father.

2. The term "law" here generally refers to the tyranny of the Smoke Monster but also to the rules of the island; for example, Jacob does not allow anyone to come inside his home (the statue) without invitation ("Ab Aeterno").

3. John, in turn, convinces Sawyer to carry out the act of murder.

4. Kate, Sawyer, John and Jin consider themselves on their own, estranged or abandoned by one or both parents.

Chapter 6

1. The spirit of George MacDonald, a real-life nineteenth-century author and Christian minister.

2. But in many cases, the dream resolution is ambiguous and the reader is not completely certain that the events of the story happened only in the mind of the central character.

3. See Chapter 4 for Friedrich Nietzsche's notion of the "eternal return" or time as a loop.

4. "An Occurrence at Owl Creek Bridge" is shown as a book of short stories in season two, "The Long Con."

5. The Swan Orientation film is hidden behind this book, as seen in "Orientation."

Chapter 8

1. Translated also as "useful and pleasant" (or, more literally, "sweet") from the Latin words "*utile et dulce*."

Bibliography

Lost. ABC/Disney, 2004–2010.

"Acts." In *New American Bible*, 2.17. New York: Catholic Book Publishing Company, 1992.

Adams, Richard. *Watership Down*. New York: Avon Books, 1975.

Aeschylus. *Agamemnon*. Edited by John Dewar Denniston and Denys Page. Oxford: Clarendon Press, 1957.

Alighieri, Dante. *The Inferno of Dante Alighieri*. London: J. M. Dent, 1900.

———. "Project Gutenberg Etext of Dante's Inferno (Divine Comedy)." *Plano Libraries*. August 1997. Available from: www.planolibraries.org/books/Inferno.pdf (accessed June 10, 2010).

Allen, Graham. *Intertextuality*. The New Critical Idiom. London: Routledge, 2000.

Aquinas, St. Thomas. "Free-will." In *The Summa Theologica of St. Thomas Aquinas*, by St. Thomas Aquinas, translated by Fathers of the English Dominican Province, 83.1., 1920.

Asbee, Sue. *Twayne's English Authors Series*. Boston, MA: Twayne Publishers, 1991.

Asimov, Isaac. "The Red Queen's Race." In *The Early Asimov; or, Eleven Years of Trying*, by Isaac Asimov. Garden City, NY: Doubleday, 1972.

Askwith, Ivan. "'Do You Even Know Where This Is Going?': *Lost*'s Viewers and Narrative Premeditation." In *Reading Lost*, by Roberta Pearson, 159–180. New York: I. B. Taurus, 2009.

Austin, Michael. "What do Jack and Locke Owe Their Fathers?" In *Lost and Philosophy: The Island Has Its Reasons*, edited by Sharon M. Kaye. Malden, MA: Blackwell Publishing, 2008.

Bakhtin, M. M. *Problems of Dostoevsky's poetics*. [Ann Arbor, Mich.]: Ardis, 1973.

Barthelme, Donald. *The Dead Father*. New York: Penguin Books, 1975.

Baum, L. Frank. "The Wonderful Wizard of Oz." *The Gutenberg Project*. July 1, 2008. Available from: www.gutenberg.org/files/55/55-h/55-h.htm (accessed January 15, 2010).

Beckett, Samuel. *Waiting for Godot*. New York: Grove Press, 1954.

Bierce, Ambrose. "An Occurrence at Owl Creek Bridge." In *The Civil War Short*

Stories of Ambrose Bierce, by Ernest J. Hopkins, 45–53. Lincoln, NE: University of Nebraska Press, 1970.

Blake, William. *The Marriage of Heaven and Hell* (first published c. 1794). New York: Dover, 1994.

Blume, Judy. *Are You There God? It's Me, Margaret.* Englewood Cliffs, NJ: Bradbury Press, 1970.

Bonetto, Sandra. "No Exit From the Island: A Sartrean Analysis of *Lost*." In *Lost and Philosophy: The Island Has Its Reasons*, edited by Sharon M. Kaye. Malden, MA: Blackwell Publishing, 2008.

Bowles, Paul. *The Sheltering Sky.* New York: New Directions, 1949.

Bradbury, Ray. "A Sound of Thunder." In *The Stories of Ray Bradbury*, by Ray Bradbury. New York: Knopf, 1980.

Bradner, Liesl. "The books of 'Lost' and TV-inspired book clubs." *Jacket Copy* (*LA Times*), March 19, 2009. Available from: latimesblogs.latimes.com/jacketcopy/2009/03/literature-lost.html (accessed August 18, 2010).

Calvin, John. *Institutes of the Christian Religion.* Peabody, MA: Hendrickson Publishers, 2008.

Campbell, Joseph. *The Hero with a Thousand Faces* (3rd edn). Novato, CA: New World Library, 2008.

Carroll, Lewis. *Alice's Adventures in Wonderland and Through the Looking-Glass.* New York: Modern Library, 2002.

Castaneda, Carlos. *A Separate Reality.* New York: Simon and Shuster, 1971.

Childers, Joseph and Gary Hentzi. "Causal Determinism." In *The Columbia Dictionary of Modern Literary and Cultural Criticism*, edited by Joseph Childers and Gary Henzi. New York: Columbia University Press, 1995.

Chozick, Amy. "'Lost' on an Ending." *The Wall Street Journal.* January 21, 2010. Available from: online.wsj.com/article/SB10001424052748703837004575013182487704058.html (accessed May 5, 2010).

Christie, Agatha. *Evil Under the Sun.* New York: The Berkley Publishing Group, 1969.

"Chronicles of Narnia." *Lostpedia.* 2009. Available from: lostpedia.wikia.com/wiki/The_Chronicles_of_Narnia (accessed January 5, 2010).

Clancy, Tom. *Rainbow Six.* New York: G. P. Putnam's Sons, 1998.

Collins, Jim. "Television and Postmodernism." In *Media Studies: A Reader*, by Paul Marris and Sue Thornham, 375–385. New York: New York University Press, 2000.

Compton-Burnett, I. (Ivy). *Manservant and Maidservant.* London: Gollancz, 1972.

Conrad, Joseph. "Heart of Darkness." In *The Story and Its Writer*, edited by Ann Charters, 333–400. Boston, MA: Bedford Books of St. Martin's Press, 1995.

Coppola, Francis Ford. *Apocalypse Now.* Produced and directed by Francis Ford

Coppola. Performed by Marlon Brando, Martin Sheen and Robert Duvall. San Francisco, CA: American Zoetrope, 1979.

Cuse, Carlton and Damon Lindelof. Interview by *USA Today*. *"Lost's Take on Religion."* Edited by Eileen Rivers, May 2010.

Cussler, Clive. *Valhalla Rising*. New York: G. P. Putnam's Sons, 2001.

Defoe, Daniel. *Robinson Crusoe*. Aerie Books, 1989.

"Determinism." *Stanford Encyclopedia of Philosophy*. January 23, 2003. Available from: plato.stanford.edu/entries/determinism-causal/ (accessed February 20, 2010).

Dick, Philip K. *VALIS*. New York: Vintage Books, 1981.

Dickens, Charles. *A Tale of Two Cities*. Oxford: Oxford University Press, 1987.

——. *Our Mutual Friend*. London: Penguin Books, 1997.

Dickens, Charles and Philip M. Parker. *A Christmas Carol*. San Diego, CA: ICON Classics, 2005. Pdf e-book. Available from: www.netlibrary.com/urlapi.asp?act ion=summary&v=1&bookid=149144 (accessed August 26, 2010).

Dostoevsky, Fyodor. *Notes From Underground*. Baltimore, MD: Penguin Books, 1972.

——. *The Brothers Karamazov*. New York: Signet Classic, New American Library, 1999.

Endō, Shūsaku. *Deep River*. Translated by Van C. Gessel. New York: New Directions, 1994.

Engelking, Sandra. *"Lost, The Third Policeman* and Guerilla Ontology." In *Lost and Philosophy: The Island Has Its Reasons*, edited by Sharon M. Kaye. Malden, MA: Blackwell Publishing, 2008.

"Ephesians." In *New American Bible*, 1.11. New York: Catholic Book Publishing Company, 1992.

"Fatalism." *Stanford Encyclopedia of Philosophy*. January 21, 2010. Available from: plato.stanford.edu/entries/determinism-causal/ (accessed February 8, 2010).

Forbes, Colin. *The Stone Leopard*. New York: HarperCollins, 1984.

Freud, Sigmund. "Dostoevsky and Parricide." In *Dostoevsky: A Collection of Essays*, by Rene Wellek, 98–111. Englewood Cliffs, NJ: Prentice-Hall, 1962.

Garland, Judy. *The Wizard of Oz*. Produced by Warner Bros. family entertainment. Performed by Judy Garland, Frank Morgan, Ray Bolger, Bert Lahr, Jack Haley, Victor Fleming, Mervyn LeRoy, et al. [S.l.]: Warner Home Video, 1999.

Gifford, Sally. "More American Adults Read Literature According to New NEA Study." *National Endowment for the Arts*. January 12, 2009. Available from: www.nea.gov/news/news09/readingonrise.html (accessed March 2, 2010).

Golden, Arthur. *Memoirs of a Geisha*. New York: Alfred A. Knopf, 1997.

Golding, William. *Lord of the Flies*. New York: The Berkley Publishing Group, 1954.

——. "William Golding talks to John Carey." In *William Golding: The Man and His Books*, by John Carey. London: Faber and Faber, 1986.

Hailey, Arthur. *Hotel*. New York: The Berkley Publishing Group, 2000.

Haley, Alex. *Roots*. Garden City, NY: Doubleday, 1976.

Hamilton, Edith. *Mythology*. New York: Little, Brown and Company, 1969.

Hawking, Stephen. *A Brief History of Time*. New York: Bantam Books, 1996.

Hawking, Stephen with Leonard Mlodinow. *A Briefer History of Time*. New York: Bantam Dell, 2005.

Heinlein, Robert A. "By His Bootstraps." *XS4ALL*. Edited by Martin Pot. First published October, 1943 in *Astounding Science Fiction*. Available from: www.xs4all.nl/~pot/scifi/byhisbootstraps.html (accessed April 1, 2010).

——. *Stranger in a Strange Land*. New York: Putnam, 1961.

——. *The Fantasies of Robert A. Heinlein*. New York: Tor, 1999. Print.

Heller, Joseph. *Catch-22*. New York: Laurel, 1990.

Hickam, Homer. *The Coalwood Way*. New York: Bantam Dell, 2000.

Higdon, David Leon. "A Revision and a Gloss." In *H. G. Wells's Perennial Time Machine*, edited by George Edgar Slusser, Patrick Parrinder and Daniele Chatelain, 177–187. Athens, GA: University of Georgia Press, 2001.

Hilton, James. *Lost Horizon*. New York: Pocket Books, 1960.

Hinton, S. E. *The Outsiders*. New York: Viking Press, 1967.

Hoag, Tami. *Dark Horse*. New York: Bantam Books, 2002.

Hodgson, William Hope. *Captain Gault: Being the Exceedingly Private Log of a Sea-Captain*. London: Eveleigh Nash, 1917.

Hoffer, Eric. *The True Believer: Thoughts on the Nature of Mass Movements*. New York: Perennial Classics, 1951.

Hollingdale, R. J. *Nietzsche: The Man and his Philosophy*. New York: Cambridge University Press, 1999.

Homer. *The Odyssey*. Translated by Samuel Butler. Roslyn: Walter J. Black, 1944.

——. *The Odyssey*. Translated by Robert Fagles. New York: Penguin Books, 1996.

Huxley, Aldous. *Island*. New York: HarperCollins, 1962.

Isaacs, Susan. *After All These Years*. New York: HarperCollins, 1993.

James, Henry. *The Turn of the Screw*. New York: Bedford/St. Martin's, 2004.

Jenkins, Henry. *Convergence Culture: Where Old and New Media Collide*. New York: NYU Press, 2006.

Jensen, Jeff. "Daddy Dearest." *Entertainment Weekly*. May 16, 2007. Available from: www.ew.com/ew/article/0,,1550612_20250233_20038982,00.html (accessed February 15, 2010).

"Job." In *New American Bible*. New York: Catholic Book Publishing Company, 1992.

"John." In *New American Bible*, 149. New York: Catholic Book Publishing, 1992.

Jones, Steven E. "Dickens on Lost: Text, Paratext, Fan-based Media." *Wordsworth Circle*, Vol. 38, No. 1/2 (Winter, 2007): 71–77.

Joyce, James. *Ulysses*. New York: Vintage Books, 1986.

Jung, C. G. *The Undiscovered Self: With Symbols and the Interpretation of Dreams*. Bollingen Series, 20. Princeton, NJ: Princeton University Press, 1990.

Kaye, Sharon M. (ed.) *Lost and Philosophy: The Island has its Reasons*. Malden, MA: Blackwell Publishing, 2008.

Kerouac, Jack. *On the Road*. New York: Viking, 1997.

Keveney, Bill. "Cuse, Lindelof shared an 'incredible journey' with 'Lost." *USA Today*. May 20, 2010. Available from: www.usatoday.com/life/television/ news/2010-05-18-lostcuselindelof18_ST_N.htm (accessed June 29, 2010).

Keyes, Daniel. *Flowers for Algernon*. New York: Harcourt, Brace and World, 1966.

Kierkegaard, Søren. *Fear and Trembling; Repetition*. Translated by Howard V. Hong and Edna H. Hong. Princeton, NJ: Princeton University Press, 1983.

King, Stephen. *Carrie*. New York: Doubleday, 1974.

——. *The Shining*. New York: Doubleday, 1977.

——. *The Stand*. New York: Doubleday, 1978.

——. *On Writing*. New York: Scribner, 2000.

——. "The Symbolic Language of Dreams." In *Dreams and Inward Journeys*, edited by Jon and Marjorie Ford, 17–23. New York: Pearson Education, 2004.

Knox, Bernard. "The date of the *Oedipus Tyrannus* of Sophocles," *The American Journal of Philology*, Vol. 77, No. 2 (1956): 133–147.

Kristeva, Julia and Kelly Oliver. *The Portable Kristeva*. New York: Columbia University Press, 2002.

LaHaye, Tim F. and Jerry B. Jenkins. *Left Behind: A Novel of the Earth's Last Days*. Wheatonville, IL: Tyndale House Publishers, 2005.

Lang, Michelle. "*Lost* as the Neo-Baroque." *Lost Studies*. Available from: loststudies.com/1.3/neobaroque.html (accessed August 25, 2010).

Lavery, David. "The Allusions of Television." *Flow TV*. January 26, 2006. Available from: flowtv.org/2006/01/the-allusions-of-television/ (accessed May 20, 2010).

Lee, Harper. *To Kill a Mockingbird*. Philadelphia, PA: Lippincott, 1960.

Lescroart, John. *The Oath*. New York: Dutton, 2002.

Lewis, C. S. *The Great Divorce: A Dream*. London: Geoffrey Bles, Centenary Press, 1945.

Lewis, C. S. and Pauline Baynes. *The Chronicles of Narnia*. New York: HarperCollins, 1994.

Lindelof, Damon. *The Lost Book Club*. Produced by Buena Vista Home Entertainment. Performed by Damon Lindelof. Buena Vista Home Entertainment, 2007.

——. Interview by Sean Carroll. "The Island Paradox: Executive producers Carlton Cuse and Damon Lindelof ponder order, chaos, and time travel with physicist Sean Carroll." *Wired Magazine*, April 19, 2010.

LOST Books Challenge. 2009. Available from: lostbookschallenge.blogspot.com/ (accessed June 1, 2010).

Lostpedia (A Lost Wikia). Available from: lostpedia.wikia.com/wiki/Main_Page (accessed May 10, 2010).

Mathewes, Jeffrey. "The Manichaean Body in *The Third Policeman:* or Why Joe's Skin Is Scaly." *The Modern Word.* Available from: www.themodernword.com/ scriptorium/obrien_mathewes.pdf (accessed January 3, 2010).

McDowell, Malcolm. *A Clockwork Orange.* Directed by Stanley Kubrick. Performed by Malcolm McDowell, Patrick Magee, and Anthony Burgess. Warner Home Video, 1983.

Melville, Herman. *Moby Dick; or The White Whale.* New York: New American Library, 1961.

Merritt, Abraham and Lynette Porter. *The Moon Pool.* New York: The Overlook Press, 2008.

Mittel, Jason. "Lost in a Great Story: Evaluation in Narrative Television." In *Reading Lost,* edited by Roberta Pearson, 119–138. London: I. B. Taurus and Co., 2009.

Nabokov, Vladimir. *Laughter in the Dark.* Indianapolis, IN, and New York, NY: Bobbs-Merrill, 1938.

Nafisi, Azar. *Reading Lolita in Tehran.* New York: Random House, 2003.

Ndalianis, Angela. *Neo-Baroque Aesthetics and Contemporary Entertainment.* Cambridge: MIT Press, 2004.

——. "Lost in Genre: Chasing the White Rabbit to Find a White Polar Bear." In *Reading Lost,* edited by Roberta Pearson, 181–197. New York: I.B.Taurus, 2009.

New American Bible. New York: Catholic Book Publishing Company, 1992.

Newlin, George. *Understanding* A Tale of Two Cities: *A Student Casebook to Issues, Sources, and Historical Documents.* Greenwood Press "Literature in context" series. Westport, CT: Greenwood Press, 1998.

Nietzsche, Friedrich. *Thus Spoke Zarathustra.* London: Penguin Books, 1969.

——. *The Gay Science.* Edited by Bernard Williams. Translated by Josefine Nauckhoff and Adrian Del Caro. Cambridge: Cambridge University Press, 2001.

O'Brien, Flann. *The Third Policeman.* Chicago, IL: Dalkey Archive Press, 1967.

O'Connor, Flannery. "Everything That Rises Must Converge." In *The Story and Its Writer,* edited by Ann Charters, 1037–1048. Boston, MA: Bedford Books of St. Martin's Press, 1995.

Oromaner, Marc. *The Myth of Lost.* New York: iUniverse, 2008.

Orwell, George. *Animal Farm.* New York: Harcourt, Brace, 1946.

——. "Charles Dickens." In *A Tale of Two Cities: Dickens's Revolutionary Novel*, edited by Ruth F. Glancy. Boston, MA: Twayne Publishers, 1991.

Patterson, Brett Chandler. "Redemption on the Island of Second Chances." In *Lost and Philosophy: The Island Has Its Reasons*, edited by Sharon M. Kaye. Malden, MA: Blackwell Publishing, 2008.

Percy, Walker. *Lancelot*. New York: Farrar, Straus and Giroux, 1977.

Perrault, Charles. "Bluebeard." In *The Blue Fairy Book*, edited by Andrew Lang. New York: Dover Press, 1965.

Phillips, Gary. *High Hand*. New York: Kensington Publishing, 2000.

Plath, Sylvia. *Ariel: Poems by Sylvia Plath*. London: Faber and Faber, 1965.

——. *The Colossus and Other Poems*. London: Faber and Faber 1967.

Porter, Lynette, David Lavery and Hillary Robson. *Lost's Buried Treasures*. Naperville: Sourcebooks, 2007.

Post, Chad. "'Lost' Premiere: How Thomas Pynchon's 'The Crying of Lot 49' Explains The Series." *Wall Street Journal*. February 2, 2010. Available from: blogs.wsj.com/speakeasy/2010/02/02/how-thomas-pynchons-the-crying-of-lot-49-explains-lost/ (accessed June 25, 2010).

——. Interview by Sarah Clarke Stuart. Phone interview (March 24, 2010).

Potok, Chaim. *The Chosen*. New York: Simon and Schuster, 1967.

Pūrjavādī, Nasrollah and Peter Lamborn Wilson (translators). *Kings of Love: the Poetry and History of the Ni'Matullāhī Sufi Order*. Tehran: Imperial Iranian Academy of Philosophy, 1978.

Rand, Ayn. *The Fountainhead*. Chicago, IL: Sears Readers Club, 1943.

Reader's Digest. *Mysteries of the Ancient Americas: The New World Before Columbus*. Pleasantville, NY: Reader's Digest Association, 1986.

Redford, Donald B. *The Ancient Gods Speak: A Guide to Egyptian Religion*. Oxford: Oxford University Press, 2002.

Ridgeon, Lloyd (ed). *Major World Religions: From Their Origins to the Present*. London: RoutledgeCurzon, 2003.

"Romans." In *New American Bible*, 8.29–30. New York: Catholic Book Publishing Company, 1992.

Rushdie, Salman. *Haroun and the Sea of Stories*. New York: Granta Books in association with Viking, 1990.

Ryan, Maureen. "The Watcher." *Chicago Tribune*. January 14, 2007. Available from: featuresblogs.chicagotribune.com/entertainment_tv/2007/01/lost_producers_.html (accessed February 28, 2010).

de Saint-Exupéry, Antoine. *The Little Prince*. Translated by Katherine Woods. New York: Harcourt, Brace and World, 1943.

Sartre, Jean-Paul. *Being and Nothingness*. New York: Washington Square Press, 1943.

——. *No Exit and Three Other Plays*. New York: Vintage Books, 1976.

Sendak, Maurice. Interview by Bill Moyers. "Maurice Sendak: *Where the Wild Things Are.*" PBS. 2004. Available from: www.pbs.org/now/arts/sendak.html (accessed August 26, 2010).

Shah, Idries. *Caravan of Dreams.* London: The Octagon Press, 1968.

Shakespeare, William. "The Tragical History of Hamlet Prince of Denmark." In *The Complete Pelican Shakespeare,* edited by Stephen Orgel and A. R. Braunmuller, 1337–1391. New York: Penguin Books, 2002.

Silverberg, Robert. *The Mirror of Infinity: A Critics' Anthology of Science Fiction.* New York: Harper and Row, 1970.

Skinner, B. F. *Beyond Freedom and Dignity.* New York: Knopf, 1971.

Steinbeck, John. *Of Mice and Men.* New York: Covici-Friede, 1937.

——. *The Pearl.* New York: Viking Press, 1947.

Stowe, Harriet Beecher. *Uncle Tom's Cabin.* Oxford: Oxford University Press, 1998.

Stuart, Sarah Clarke. *Books and Lost.* Survey, Polldaddy, 2010.

——. "Has Lost Inspired You to Read a New Book?" *DocArzt & Friends Lost Blog.* May 5, 2010. Available from: www.docarzt.com/Lost/Lost-news/has-Lost-inspired-you-to-read-a-new-book/#comments (accessed May 13, 2010).

Sutherland, Robert. *Putting God on Trial: The Biblical Book of Job, A Literary, Legal and Philosophical Study.* Victoria, BC: Trafford Publishing, 2004.

Sutin, Lawrence. *Philip K. Dick Bibliography.* 2003. Available from: www.philipkdick.com/aa_biography.html (accessed May 15, 2010).

Terras, Victor. *A Karamazov Companion.* Translated by Constance Garnett. Madison, WI: University of Wisconsin Press, 2002.

"The Third Policeman." *Lostpedia.* 2005. Available from: lostpedia.wikia.com/wiki/The_Third_Policeman (accessed June 25, 2010).

Thomas, P. L. *Reading, Learning, Teaching Kurt Vonnegut: Confronting the Text, Confronting the World.* New York: Peter Lang, 2006.

Troup, Gary. *Bad Twin.* New York: Hyperion, 2006.

Tuerk, Richard. *Oz in Perspective: Magic and Myth in the L. Frank Baum Books.* Jefferson, NC: MacFarland & Co., 2007.

Vees-Gulani, Susanne. "Diagnosing Billy Pilgrim: A Psychiatric Approach to Kurt Vonnegut's *Slaughterhouse-Five.*" *Critique,* Vol. 44, No. 2 (Winter 2003): 175–185.

Verne, Jules. *Jules Verne: Narratives of Modernity.* Liverpool: Liverpool University Press, 2000.

——. *Survivors of the Chancellor.* Lenox, MA: Hard Press, 2006.

Vonnegut, Kurt. *Slaughterhouse-Five.* New York: The Dial Press, 1969.

Watkins, Steven. "Teilhard de Chardin's View of Diminishment and the Late Stories of Flannery O'Connor." PhD dissertation, University of Texas, Arlington, 2005.

Wells, H. G. *The Island of Dr. Moreau.* New York: Bantam Classics, 1994.

———. *The Time Machine*. New York: Bantam Books, 2003.

Wells, H. G. and John Clute. *The Shape of Things to Come*. New York: Penguin, 2006.

Winston, Diane. Interview by Krista Tippett. *TV and Parables of Our Time* (July 16, 2009). Available from: speakingoffaith.publicradio.org/ programs/2009/tv/ (accessed August 26, 2010).

Woods, Stuart. *Dirty Work*. New York: Signet, New American Library, 2003.

Wright, Peter. *Hindsight*. New York: iUniverse, 2005.

Index